REIGN

16 secrets from 6 Queens to rule your world
with clarity, connection & sovereignty

Caroline Hurry

HYGGE BOOKS

ISBN:
978-0-620-98494-2

Cover design: Rebecacovers
Layout: Graphic Design/Birgitte Berg-Munch
Fonts: Jost, Cormorant and Cinzel Decorative
Crown sketches: Caroline Morris

Library of Congress Control Number:
TXu002307091
Printed in the United States of America

DEDICATION

For Hygge Queens everywhere. May you always flow along currents of financial freedom, friendship, and care.

Thanks & Acknowledgments

Like trees in a forest joined at the roots, this book could not have been born without the ever-widening boughs of connection stretching across our realm.

First, thank you to Jacqueline, aka Oracle Girl – an embodiment of the multidimensional me "at a future time-space coordinate" – for helping me reboot my resolve every morning, with her constant encouragement; to "keep going."

Jacqueline describes herself as one of several "nodes or physical markers tackling the purity and impurity of our selves at progressively deeper levels." She infuses encouragement into her nourishing instructions from our sovereign source.

Thank you, sonic alchemist and beloved friend Wendy Leppard, for all the sound baths and for introducing me to Jacqueline's work, which resonated from the start.

Of course, who knows where anything begins? Biofield leader Eileen McKusick's research prompted me to seek out Wendy before that. Their rich insights feature in the air section.

The Scottish artist Caroline Morris, who sketched the crowns, describes Jacqueline as "my personal Mary Poppins (who) makes me feel as though I can do things and brings the medicine I need."

Jacqueline's presence, her gentle but firm encouragement, breathtaking generosity of spirit, and shining influence weave through like a golden thread. She inspired much of this book. Thank you, Jacqueline, for your continued fortifications.

Thanks also to the firestarters – all those trailblazing queens who shared their stories in the first section – Myrtle Clarke, Monica Zwolsman, Denise Bjorkman, Lois Kuhle, Lise Essberger, Esther de Villiers, Maggie Ubsdell, Cecily Guarrera, elementor Liesl Haasbroek, Zanna of Cape Town, the courageous Dr. Christiane Northrup, Shamama Artio, ordained Priestess of the Sacred Feminine and traditional healer, Nkogono Mantsielo.

The contributions of Catherine Lancaster, Mel Gouws, Jacqueline Smidt, and writer Helen Grange added emotional flow to the water section. Thank you.

I'm grateful to my family for their unswerving love – my mother, Elaine, whose timeless tale features in the water section, brother Simon for my author portrait, sister Mags for her steadfast support, and Svesken.

Scandinavian Terje Isungset's ice sounds amaze, along with New Zealand water whisperer Veda Austin's incredible research into the conscious artistry of water and ice. Pat McCabe's story reminds us to remain fluid in adversity.

The ground-breaking research of ecologists Dr. Suzanne Simard and Dr. Monica Gagliano will renew your awe of ecosystems in the earth section. Thanks to Australian cosmic warrior JC Kay, who talks to the trees and passes on their messages.

Thanks to the effervescent Dondi Dahlin for her work on the five elements in the metal section and author Leanne Babcock, who teaches women how to put themselves first.

The Danish graphic designer Birgitte Berg-Munch devised this book's beautiful design. *Tusind tak, kaere* Birgitte!

Ilse Sasser, a constant source of kind reassurance and excellent humor, helped keep me calm. You're the best, Ilsetjie!

Proofreader Lynn Whyle spared my blushes with her eagle eye, and author astrologer Linda Shaw read my manuscript and made valuable suggestions.

Thanks to authors Lana Jacobson and Janine Lazarus for their encouraging early reviews. Fearless journalist Beth Cooper Howell, author-artist Donna White, Cape Town Carrie, Aylex Cross, Nikki Rood, Bronwyn Millar, Lucille McN, and my daily walking companions, Uscha and Phillippa – thank you for your encouragement, friendship, and support.

Keyword coach David White generously shared his publishing knowledge and provided much-appreciated reassurance.

Last but not least, a big thank you to the Hygge Queens and leaf sisters who keep the currencies of care and camaraderie afloat on The Coterie. You rule!

BONUS

The heroine's journey of integrity seeks clarity, connection, and wholeness in a Western culture that often fails to uphold feminine values and can seem increasingly bewildering.

In a sisterhood of camaraderie and support, female friendships keep the currencies of care afloat. These timeless observations, humor, and wisdom from women like you in *Wit & Wisdom From The Hygge Queen Coterie* will surprise and delight.

Download your gift copy from carolinehurry.com for wry musings about human nature, life, love, menopause, and how we relate.

WIT & WISDOM
FROM THE HYGGE QUEEN COTERIE

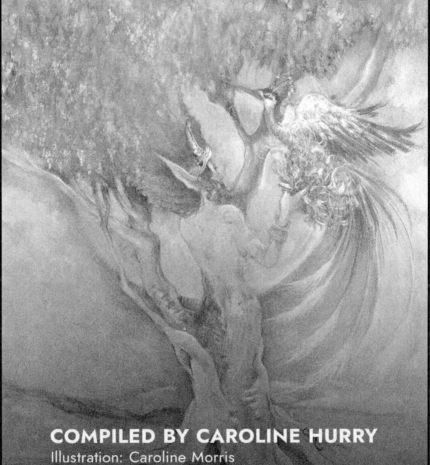

COMPILED BY CAROLINE HURRY
Illustration: Caroline Morris

A gift especially for you

Whose magical tour is it, anyway?

I began, as you do, by rubbing the sleep from my eyes. Bafflement had become my default mode; okay, *fine*, permanent abode – scoffing pickled cod on cabbage in Oslo hotels and penning airline reviews one minute; plunging Alice-like down a rabbit hole into a dystopian realm the next. *Whoosh!*

Welcome to *Le Pandemique*, a global production brought to you by – well, let's say multinational corporations with vested interests.

Wuhan's dramatic footage of folk dropping dead in the street lost its shock value when other reportage showed a corpse sneaking a crafty fag, between takes, from the body bag.[1] [2]

"Curiouser and curiouser!" [3]

Whatever the cause of the televised pandemic – bat soup slurpers in China, rogue viruses, bio weaponry, possibly 5G – international holiday jollies screeched to a halt, as did my paid assignments.

My travel website bobbed crewless like the *Mary Celeste* on an uncertain sea. So much for drinking deep from life's silver goblet.

I'd been handed a pre-colonoscopy prep after ordering a Margarita. "Drink Me," the label said.

When I did, I realized this oh-so-strange *Brave New World* landscape begged further exploration. Travel is about broadening your horizons and meeting new people, so who better to peer into a few keyholes than a curious travel scribe like Yours Truly.

To learn about a place, you can either lurk on the outskirts of tour groups to eavesdrop on the guides or get down with the locals.

I did both. I started the Coterie of Hygge Queens, an online abbey for women as bemused as me. Within this far-flung sisterhood of survivors bubbled a cornucopia of talent and artistry as we negotiated the cracks of our wavering reality. Some fought cancers, loneliness, or loss of income through Draconian regulations, while others mourned the loss

---

1   @newsraters, 2020

2   NewGrenada, 2021

3   Carroll, 2021

of partners or their youthful *joie de vivre*. They were generous enough to share their stories.

Kindness and collaboration became the new currency. I discovered what lay over the hill was not a pasture for long-forgotten mares but an infinite field of shimmering possibilities.

Connected via unseen roots, I found friends I felt I'd known forever, even though we'd never met in real life.

With the help of this supportive network, I began to eject the debris of whiny slavish corporate supporter identities – angry victims, people-pleasers, homemakers struggling to breathe within python coils of conformity. Like unwanted houseguests hogging the hot water, criticizing my cooking, rehashing tired old tales of woe, they had to go.

It was surprisingly easy – most removed themselves or stepped up their game. I thought I knew where love lay. Boy, was I wrong! Hint: It's not what the jewelry commercials say.

What can I tell you? I used to be afraid to speak my mind. Now, I put my thoughts out there because the good opinions of minions no longer concern me. I weighed 8kg more. My excess weight melted away along with the baggage of self-blame.

None of this happened overnight. Transmutation takes a little time, but it's not complicated.

All you need do is show up for yourself, bask in Mother Nature's frequency, and clear the channels for your divine source connection to shine through and nourish you.

Unequal parts memoir, self-help manual, travelogue, and occasionally unreliable map back to Mother Nature's realm, the self-revelatory journeys within these pages pertain to any woman seeking to remain sovereign in a world hellbent on subjugation.

Some call it Bliss. I call it Hygge.

Start here, if you like

One day you're the queen of the hill. The next day you're invisible. And by day, I mean decade – with the dead tucked between the C and the E. Oh, foolish, cynical me!

Cold, bleak circumstances have all but doused your inner flame. You feel like a random particle bouncing off external forces beyond your control. Sure, you followed instructions, but nothing got back to normal. Things you thought true no longer work for you. Promised rewards for compliance vanished like pre-Omicron variants.

Chin up. Regrets are futile. I, too, traversed potholed roads from one crisis to another. I got rejected, disrespected, overlooked, and undervalued. I felt too depressed to get dressed until I started springcleaning.

So you sweep the room with a glance? Yeah, that won't work here. We're talking filter changes, bridge-burning, and identity annihilation – whatever triggers despair.

Housework is about as much fun as forgetting the code to the shrieking burglar alarm. I *know*.

Rest assured, you'll hardly need to lift a finger this time. Enough, already!

Nature will undo you, ready or not.

Those who easily relinquish worn-out identities are better prepared when bombshells drop from the blue, which they'll likely continue to do. Purity, clarity, and connection open more routes into an expanded timeline.

Life through a clean window beats staring through a glass darkly. There's little to recommend the dim and murky view, but it's up to you. The more you let nature dissolve the grime, the brighter your light will shine. But, this isn't a race.

Nothing is compulsory down Introspection Avenue. We all purify at our own pace. Prepare to relinquish who you used to be.

Open the shutters – free your ghosts. The winds turn skeletons to dust. The sun thaws frozen shards of pain. Anything meant for you will remain. You're not alone. Just trust.

Old pastures morph into vibrational fields of solace and self-sufficiency along the continual purification journey as things we once took for granted fall away.

It's hard to know what's real, how to think, or what to feel in these unprecedented times. What you learn will either limit or expand your vision. The good news is you have a set of instructions inside you to bring your unique elemental frequencies into permutations of harmony and facilitate a more expansive reality.

Nature knows what to do and how to guide you. All you need do is sharpen your awareness of what it's like to be you.

Carry on as you are, if you like, but isn't the height of folly expecting new outcomes from old ways of being? What would you create if you allowed your magic to radiate?

Inside, you'll meet other queens who turned life's bombshells into bonfire fuel and set it alight.

Some lost homes, health, and husbands through death or divorce. In releasing histories, they stepped into their stories.

We found each other killing time in the Coterie – waiting for the Rapture, Ragnarok, an alien invasion – I don't know, *something*.

Recognition sparked a connection flow across cyber waves, maintaining buoyancy through break-ups, burnouts, fear, and despair.

The elemental queens and their archetypes represent me. And you, too, because you *will* find yourself in this book. We need no permission, selection, or validation to create what we choose.

The queen does not lower her vibe for anyone – the opinions of minions matter not. Are you willing to let go of the life you planned to embrace, the one waiting for you?

To paraphrase Joseph Campbell, you bring meaning to life and not the other way around, so why waste time asking the question when you are the answer?

You can align with the divine and rule your realm at any age. It's never too late. Read on if you'd like to see yourself reflected in miraculous ways. Within these pages lie shared revelations, real-life experiences, hard-won discoveries, and a sense of unity.

Grab my hand. Let's harness our butterflies and begin the transformative journey!

Contents

SECTION II

WATER 75

CHAPTER 4

CHAPTER 5

CHAPTER 6

SECTION III

AIR 115

SECTION IV
EARTH 153

SECTION V

METAL

SECTION VI

HYGGE 209

THE SIX QUEENS

FIRE QUEEN

- *Burns everything so new realities can emerge.*
- *Arises from the ashes of old paradigms.*
- *Transmutes situations and sparks herself.*

WATER QUEEN

- *Masters the stream of telepathy for emotional fluency.*
- *Dissolves worn-out identities and situations.*
- *Renegotiates relationships with ease and washes away all manipulation attempts.*

AIR QUEEN

- *Adjusts her language, fine-tunes her frequencies, wields her words with purpose, and speaks to power.*
- *Slashes through fake histories and language constructs.*
- *Sharpens her blades of discernment, recognizes patterns in prevailing societal narratives, and rewrites her scripts.*

EARTH QUEEN

- *Aligns with the Divine through Earth's magnetic energy.*
- *Grounds and embeds herself into the most potent frequency.*
- *Builds strength, stamina, and good posture.*

METAL QUEEN

- *Moves forward with courage.*
- *Applies grace under pressure.*
- *Maintains independent thought for more meticulous wisdom.*

HYGGE QUEEN

- *Welcomes silence. Rises above social conditioning.*
- *Intuits the truth, maintains her resonance, and remains regal.*
- *Expresses wisdom, strength, and sovereignty.*

SECTION I

FIRE

The first element of freedom speaks in tongues of flame that dance, ignite the heart, lick the air, or rage through a forest.

Fire reduces matter to nothing, builds mountains through volcanoes, and purifies before materializing something new.

Fiery solar energy manifests our material existence, connecting us with the other five elements via our sparks of infinity.

CHAPTER 1

TRIALS BY FIRE

*"We are volcanoes. When we women offer our experience
as our truth, as human truth, all the maps change.
There are new mountains."*
– URSULA-K-LE-GUIN

Well, it's all right for *her*, I hear you say. She had a happy childhood, a rich husband, a high-profile career, or whatever you don't have. You're lonely, widowed, retrenched, facing illness and pain. No hope for you, right?

Wrong. The women in this chapter faced these things and emerged more robust than ever.

Some share their composite experiences of ancestral wounding.

By recognizing their existence on every level of creation, they scrapped their fears and, in doing so, allowed their creative consciousness to emerge. They chose themselves.

Whether aware of any eternal presence experiencing their unique version of reality through their bodily senses or not, they continue to slash through the undergrowth of fear and set it alight.

The best example I know of someone who continues to speak out even if her voice shakes is Myrtle Clarke.

FLAMES OF INJUSTICE

Myrtle Clarke became a reluctant activist in 2010 when police raided their six-acre farm, subjected her to three humiliating strip searches, and held her partner Julian Stobbs at gunpoint for five hours – for less than a kilogram of cannabis.

Where lesser mortals may have crumbled, Myrtle and Julian sued seven government departments and set up Fields of Green for All, a non-profit organization launched to legalize the plant.

The Trial of the Plant saw victory in 2018 with the decriminalization of using, growing, and keeping cannabis for personal use in South Africa. However, Myrtle's trials were far from over.

In the early hours of Friday, July 3, 2020, thugs broke into their home and shot Julian dead in their bed, where they lay asleep. They fled with two cell phones and two laptops.

The violent abruptness of her life partner's exit meant Myrtle had somehow to find her way alone through the screaming resonance of a nightmare reality. Having never encountered anyone whose partner got murdered in their bed made her feel even lonelier.

"No matter how many podcasts or TED talks I listened to, there was this visceral hole of 'nobody understands because Julian didn't just die.' I longed to speak to someone else, but there wasn't anyone.

"Being pulled in all directions within the blackness of grief made it unbelievably hard to navigate my world, especially as the broken police system means Julian's killers remain at large.

"The police, right now, cause my biggest heartache, but I am no longer afraid. Good people disobey tyranny. The worst thing has already happened to me. The day Julian got shot in our bed, more than 50 other South Africans experienced something traumatic.

"I stand with every person who has seen their loved ones murdered as criminals run rampant with impunity. There is no justice for the hundreds of murders, rapes, and armed robberies occurring daily for ordinary people.

Myrtle continues to stand up to authoritarian bullies, defending Mother Nature and the thousands of others devastated by violence.

"I asked our police chief what he would do if his wife got shot dead next to him in their bed. He never responded."

She counts an "amazing artist and activist therapist" among her blessings and finds renewed fortitude in drawing, painting, and taking breaks in the magnificent South African bush. Myrtle is a true warrior queen who keeps going when lesser women might have thrown in the towel long ago. "I miss Julian every single day, but I will keep fighting. I won't stop until we get Fields of Green for all," she says.

BURNING BRIGHT

Neuroscientist Denise Bjorkman lost her first husband to a hijacking, the second to motor neuron disease, and her third to suicide. She reflects on coping in the aftermath.

"After each loss, exploring my identity took on a new meaning as I had to evaluate how my being had fused with my respective husbands and defined me.

"The loss of three husbands was too much. They kaleidoscoped on each other in the weeks that followed my third husband, Derek's death. At any given moment, I did not know who I was grieving.

"I lost 34 kgs in less than eight weeks. Covid had begun, so I was in isolation on a farm, 3.8 km from my nearest neighbor. We had no farmhands. I was utterly alone.

"A suicide scene is no friend to memories. In the month following Derek's death, somebody found me parked beside a road far from home and took me to a hospital. I have no memory of that week.

"My flashbacks haunt me, as does the silence in the room following the rifle shot. It's a different silence to the quiet of the countryside.

"Derek always told me that even if I were not in the room, he could hear slight movements in the house that spoke of me, and he would know I was near. Those amplified sounds were absent.

"Derek had cancer of the prostate. The costs of chemo, oncologists, physicians, surgery, and hospitalization had hollowed our coffers. Derek had no medical aid, having been in perfect health before his diagnosis. I was the breadwinner and worked overseas eight days a month while he ran the house and farm.

"Living on a farm in paradise – our *Belle Epoque*, as Derek and I named it - with an uncluttered view of the Magaliesberg and the biosphere hills helped clear my mind. When I had decisions to make, I would climb the mountains and look to the horizon.

"We had spent almost 18 years lying on the grass at night looking at vast open champagne skies, no pollution, just the odd wayward satellite ambling under the sparkle.

"On the flip side, Nature was both foe and friend, infusing so many memories of him. Every night, we fed a mongoose family that brought their young for us to see and showed them where to find food.

"We allowed swallows' nests in the large enclosed patio of our bedroom, watched their habits daily, and bore witness to the fledgling maiden flights. They left for overseas around Easter and returned end of September. We kept our windows open for them.

"We discussed books long into the night. We often cleared our bedroom deck, prepared a silver-platter supper, and shuffle danced to The Platters, Nat King Cole, Vera Lynn, the Ink Spots, and Sinatra. Derek could rock like no other. We played Little Richard, Bill Hayley and the Comets, Elvis, and Tina Turner at full blast. How the Golden Valley echoed, but we had no neighbors to complain.

"After Derek shot himself, my strengths, coping mechanisms, resilience, or any sense of poise or balance deserted me. His presence was ubiquitous. He had left notes everywhere to tell me how to manage the farm, a mammoth job.

"I wept day and night. Howled would be more accurate. I suffered from aloneness. I missed being loved, kissed, and held. Grief came in crippling chest pains, but I refused anti-depressants. I needed to feel. As I regressed into fetal positions, our three dogs provided some solace, and John Bowlby's book, *Loss*, offered many of the answers I needed to continue.

"I used Facebook to help regain my sanity. So long as I engaged my brain, I could not let my flooding emotions - self-pity, loss, abandonment, and blinding grief overwhelm me.

"Reading, shared music, research, the countryside, and being hyper-connected on the Coterie kept me together. My children, who live far from me, contact me often.

"I read a lot of poetry and turned my collection of global art movies into a visual sanctuary."

Ashes to ashes:

Monica Zwolsman (nee Nicolson, Oosterbroek, and Hilton-Barber) lost her first husband, Ken Oosterbroek, to a sniper bullet and her second, Steve Hilton-Barber, to a heart attack. Not long after Steve's death, she found her 16-month-old son, Benjamin, dead in his cot.

"I won't allow the worst of my past – all the heartbreak, tragedy, and sadness – to define the rest of my life.

"Grief, loss, love, and family can be challenging to untangle, especially when others rummage through my baggage, too, picking up bits and returning them to me.

"When they neither want to keep nor let go of family albums, they give them to me. It's hard not to accept treasured shared memories, but a deep nostalgia coupled with the love for people I've known can flood my body and overwhelm me.

"All it takes is a smell, a photo, a social media comment, a piece of music, or just a corny meme. Bitter-sweet but cherished memories instill a sense of warm gratitude that helps me feel less afraid, less lonely, and more human.

"As they drift through the neighborhood of my headspace, I've grown to see grey rather than clear-cut black and white areas.

"I'm more tolerant. When I was young and opinionated, decisions were clear-cut and easy to make. Now they're more complicated.

"I can't change the past. No amount of wishing can, and I'm at peace with that. I have no regrets. Dwelling on what I could have done is pointless. Revisiting misfortune or mistakes is a significant barrier to happiness.

"Life is random. Genetics, events, and social conditioning determine our destinies. Either way, we have little control over what happens, so I believe in jumping into the flow and riding the rapids to the end.

"When I contemplate the array of possibilities, colors, and scenarios before me, it's easy to get trapped in a quagmire of options.

"Today, I'm gentler with myself. Emotional extremes exhaust me, and I focus on conserving my energy.

"My life path led me to Australia, where I live with my two wonderful sons. I could not love them more. Like the plasma in a lava lamp, I continue to move and morph shape in response to heat. My essence remains. I keep breathing and moving on!"

Monica's natural life force keeps her strong.

DOUSING THE EMBERS

Lois Kuhle and her husband Ken bought a game farm in KwaZulu-Natal after leaving Kenya in 2000. They inherited two female tigers saved from a circus in Mozambique and released bushpigs, caracals, jackals, tortoises, and other rehabilitated wild animals. Lois and Ken were on a road trip when he died of a heart attack in the car.

"Ken was 57 to my 35 – I was half his age plus seven. He told my mum he would be the happiest man alive if he could have just ten years with me. He died in our tenth year together.

"Not long after we arrived from Kenya, we discovered the farm we'd bought had a land claim on it, so our first five years in South Africa were frustrating, exhausting, traumatic, unsettling, and fateful. In Pongola, Ken segued from adoring to complex.

"I could do nothing right. He snapped at me constantly. I felt isolated and on shaky ground with him.

"We were driving through the Natal Midlands looking for somewhere new to live. There was a winter chill in the air. The sun had just set. Suddenly, Ken clutched his chest. Within a minute, he was dead.

"I had no idea where we were. I kept driving, came across the Midlands Inn, and ran in screaming like a mad thing. What a nightmare!

"The ambulance team refused to take him. I had to drive him to a hospital an hour away for a doctor to declare him dead so that undertakers could collect him. It was surreal.

"At 45, I found myself alone on the farm in Pongola, with Government Land Claim issues to resolve. Not a heap of fun.

"I felt despondent, but I had to pull myself together. My tigers and croc-odiles were hungry. I had to source dead cows and chickens.

"Knowing I had to vacate the farm within three months because of the land claim gave me a sense of purpose even as the tragedy of everything consumed me.

"I wafted around in an alcoholic haze – no point in leaving all our stock behind – before packing up and heading for Durban and my new life.

"When we first settled in Zululand, my isolation led me to deepen my connection with the bush. We released more than 400 animals back into the wild, and even though Ken did not come with an instruction manu-al, he also introduced me to one of Nature's most magnificent habitats.

"We established a Trust working with neighboring communities. I'm still involved with this project 20 years down the line, but I can no longer watch anything to do with animals on TV. My chest tightens. Anxiety squeezes my heart.

"I recall the moment I allowed myself to drop my sense of guilt and remorse. It felt exhilarating. Now I tell anyone in mourning that you'll find yourself living for so much more when you can release past attach-ments, including who you were."

Fanning the flames

Nature is ruthless and always right. Fire will burn whatever Nature con-siders superfluous, whether you're ready or not. The best you can do is work with your inner Fire as it arises.

My menopausal journey was a hot, prickly affair that left me ill-tem-pered and apt to snap. Other women describe their brains as "catching fire" during menopause. Dr. Christiane Northrup, a board-certified OB/GYN, says that's when "many, if not most," touch and feel their anger for the first time.[1]

The triggers or events that evoke the rage are never new, but "our willingness and energy to acknowledge and express that anger can be the first step toward much-needed, often long-overdue change in our lives."

---

1 Northrup, 2021

Nobody knows that better than Lise Essberger, lodge owner, horse whisperer, fire dancer, and poi teacher. She attracted fires like sun rays on glass – two of her homes burned to the ground – until she gave vent to an inner fury that had simmered for decades.

Lise had to grow up fast and deal with loss early. When she was just two, her father left her mother, Margaret, to raise her alone and put her through school.

Her life came crashing down one Monday morning in June 1987 when Margaret's jilted ex-boyfriend entered their property and shot her in the head before shooting himself.

Brushing her teeth when the first gunshot shattered the quiet suburban morning, Lise's stomach turned to jelly as she walked out of the bathroom in a trance.

"I did not want to face my worst fear. My mother – my everything – lay bleeding on the ground. I covered her with a blanket and waited for the ambulance."

A scan at the hospital revealed massive brain damage. The once laughing vital Margaret had no motor functions left. The doctors asked to harvest her organs. Lise signed consent, her heart in a million pieces.

"I had to let her go. It was the hardest thing ever. I wanted to hide like a hurt animal, but I refused sedatives to cope. Why prolong the pain? There were obligations to fulfill, deadlines to meet."

Aged 24, Lise took over her mother's publishing company with a staff of 12. Seven years later, she sold it, bought land spanning the Crocodile River within a nature reserve, built four thatched dwellings, and started Lethabo Estate, a guest lodge that continues to thrive.

Lise took up fire dancing at age 45, mesmerizing audiences from Sun City to Seychelles with her spirited performances.

"Dancing with fire burned away my inhibitions and gave me the confidence to perform. The fire expressed itself through me as though we were the same entity.

"After Margaret's death, I had shied away from conflict, but my simmering internal rage needed a valve. Fire dancing sparked me. I came alive with the primal drama of it all."

Then menopause kicked in.

"I felt red to white-hot, and that was just my anger levels. Fires broke out around me all the time.

"I'd go to Cape Town, and a forest fire would rage across the mountain. The veld around my farm kept burning. I felt jinxed.

"One friend refused to be near me in case I 'started' another fire!"

Lightning struck one of Lise's thatched dwellings and burned it to the ground. Shortly afterward, bales of hay stacked too close to the generator caught alight, razing a second abode.

Finally, Lise connected the external fires to the purifying nullification of suppressed rage and anguish that had held her back for years.

"I was able to move from unconscious exploding to harnessing my inner fire. I learned to welcome its fiery ruthlessness, knowing it was blazing a trail to something newer. I even rebuilt my homes in a better style afterward.

"When I learned not just to face but embrace my anguish as an agent of transformation, Nature instilled a renewed appreciation for all her elements.

"I purified the pain and rose like a regenerated Phoenix from the ashes when I let the fire empower me.

"I named my favorite horse Phoenix to remind me daily of Nature's benevolence and strength.

"The elements are everything in life. I have an idea (Air) and get emotional about it (Water). I take action (Fire) towards it and (Earth) it into being. It's how we all create.

"My horses are magnificent teachers too, resonating as they do with Nature's golden frequency. They intuit and easily sense dissonance, inauthenticity, hunger, and despair. It's how horses help people overcome all kinds of emotional blockages.

"When you set intentions with clarity and focus, they *will* manifest. I've proved it to myself time and again."

Today, Lise raises beautiful Nguni cows, works with her beloved horses, and plants labyrinths of organic vegetables on the estate. Thanks to the catalyst of Fire, Lise now negotiates her life with a daily sense of joy and appreciation.

RAGING INFERNO

Esther de Villiers and her husband Gerhard were at a restaurant when the worst wildfire in South African history began to billow across the mountain on June 7, 2017. As they watched wild winds whipping up flames that would cause a financial loss of $221million, they assumed their beloved dogs Milo and Bennie would head to their favorite beach playground.[1]

"We had fed them and ensured our access gate to Robberg Beach was open before overnighting in a hotel with our two children, Ella and Henri. We listened with growing alarm to reports of the fire's path. Little did we know that only ashes and bits of the brick walls Gerhard's grandparents constructed in the mid-1950s would remain of our home by sunrise the next day.

"Scattered rain fell in the night, so the following morning, hoping the fire might be under control, we went to check on our home and round up the dogs. Unable to see anything through the haze on the beach amid the howling wind, I walked back to the car while Gerhard tried to access our property from the beach service road. I heard the pops of gas bottles exploding and just knew that they were ours. We had been living off the grid, relying solely on solar power, gas, and a backup generator, since 1997.

"Social media was abuzz with reports of pets reuniting with their owners, so we were still confident we would reunite with our beloved dogs."

The fire had displaced thousands of animals. Film editor Maggie Ubsdell, who also lost her entire home to the Knysna fire, encountered a rare caracal in the burned veld seeking water right next to her.

"I'll never forget seeing that. I lost my art collected over decades, but I was more upset about my missing kitten," she recalls.

Maggie found her kitten seven days later. Sadly, Esther and her family were not as lucky.

---

1   Maitre, 2017

"When we visited the still-smoldering rubble of our property on Sunday, not a single object had withstood the heat. Even our big black three-legged cast-iron pot had melted into the shape of a Dali still-life.

"On seeing a weird rubbery blob amid the debris, where the shower used to be, I said to my friend Kath in my best French accent: '*C'est un monstre!*'

"Later that morning, I learned the 'monster lump' was the remains of Milo. Bennie's charred remnants were nearby.

"The fireman said the dogs would have died of smoke inhalation before the flames reached them. It was scant consolation. How had they gotten back into the house?

"Dogs, we learned, will run into a burning house in search of familiar surrounds. Cats – like Maggie's kitten – will flee. We surmised the wind had blown out the glass doors and windows. Perhaps the dogs perceived it as a safe place.

"Maggie, and others who suffered substantial losses in the same fire, kept me semi-sane in the following months. I discovered community in the collective loss. At the time, I co-owned our local newspaper. Writing and editing other stories about the fire helped me feel less alone.

"In the years that followed, we moved from friends' homes to fully-furnished rentals and back again. A mining magnate availed his magnificent holiday home to us for five months – one of the many acts of kindness that softened the blow of our losses.

"My regular beach rituals – sea swims and barefoot walks as the surf washes over my sandy toes, irrespective of the weather, remind me to be grateful for today. I continue to thank my lucky stars for the support of wonderful people."

Defiance as a superPower

Cecily Guarrera (61) of Wellington, New Zealand, was given three months to live after being diagnosed with an incurable form of Stage 4 lung cancer – six years ago.

"My mother died of lung cancer when I was just 16 – within three months of the diagnosis. For decades, it hung over my head like the

Sword of Damocles. Around the time of her death, I got addicted to cigarettes. A woman once told me: 'You smoke out of defiance.'

"That's so true. I do. When Mum died, my teenage self was so heart-broken; I just wanted to be with her. So I took to smoking, not caring whether I lived or not. I'll never forget walking to the corner café in Groenkloof, Pretoria, where I grew up and the cafe owner telling me I owed him money for a pack of cigarettes my mother had bought.

"She was languishing in the clinic across the road. I felt horrified. In her dying days, Mum had to cross the busy street in her hospital night-gown and slippers to buy fags because the nurses would confiscate them. She was on her way out. Why couldn't she have a little respite?

"Around six years ago, my coughing got so bad I had to sleep upright. A specialist found a big cancerous mass in my lungs – the same thing that killed Mum. The oncologist gave me three months to live – six at the most.

"I thought: 'Oh fuck, I need longer than that!'

"Should-haves, would-haves, and could-haves were no longer rele-vant, including smoking. I would not stress myself further by giving that up too.

"Instead, I thought about what I did want – to return to South Africa to say goodbye to my family. My son was 22. I wanted more time with him too.

"I searched my soul for how I had manifested this. The toxic envi-ronment of my work at a global organization run by evil people was causing me untold grief, stress, and resentment. Now, I had the evidence to prove my job was killing me. I gathered the remaining shreds of my sanity and bailed.

"Thinking I'd soon be dead, I had a Living Funeral with a crowd-fund-ing Facebook page. Messages of support flooded in. So many friends, cli-ents, children I'd taught (and their parents) expressed their gratitude for what I had meant to them. Realizing I had made a difference in many people's lives made it easier for me to let go.

"I refused chemo, but the oncologist said if I wanted to fly from New Zealand to South Africa via Singapore, I'd have to consent to at least one course of radiation, so what could I do? I was determined to say my goodbyes.

"Four weeks after a few hellish radiation sessions requiring massive doses of morphine to deal with indescribable pain, I flew to Cape Town.

"After a barefoot walk along the beach and a good night's sleep, I awoke the following day to cooing turtle doves and realized I had no pain for the first time in a long while.

"I soaked up Vitamin D in the abundant sunshine, smoked, and walked barefoot on the beach every day. A herbalist prescribed cannabis oil. Three weeks later, I felt a million times better.

"I felt so vital that I resolved to continue treating myself with cannabis oil instead of enduring chemo or more radiation on my return to New Zealand.

"Before I left for South Africa, I was the frailest in my Wellington cancer support group. The other members were extra kind to me, thinking I'd be the first to go. They opted for chemotherapy. I watched them each get sicker and die. I'm the only survivor from the group.

"With my finances at a low ebb, I had to trust the universe. I spent all my savings on quality cannabis oil, Phoenix Tears. My dismayed oncologist never stopped urging me into conventional chemotherapy.

"I continued to smoke, which caused such anger in one of my friends she stopped speaking to me. Trying to explain that my strength lies in my mental, emotional and spiritual attitudes cut no ice. I made a few dietary changes. I juiced every morning – perhaps to counteract the smoking!

"I couldn't face more work after all the angst of my previous job. Since I'm in the change management business, I embarked on a road trip around the country, living out of a suitcase, and bartering with friends en route. I'd pay them a small rent and tutor their children or provide value in a way they needed.

"Living in limbo, I dropped all my expectations. I had no money. My goal every day was to 'feel joy' with the simplest things. A month before the 2020 Covid lockdown, I found a bedsit and a part-time teaching job.

Today, I'm okay. I don't dwell on dark shadows. I like to live in my 'happy place.' Painting has been a way to express and release my anguish. I sold a few 'dark works,' but it's not what I want to put into the world. Art is how I channel spirit into matter. It brings meaning to my life.

"Like Nature, you have to destroy and annihilate to create. I had to let Nature nullify the parts of my life that were killing me. Having outlived my oncologist's three-month prognosis by six years and counting, I asked him why he refused to consider sunshine, juicing, and cannabis oil viable alternative treatments to chemo. He declined to answer.

"Now, I spend as much time in the sunshine as possible. There's not much of it in New Zealand, but I also seek thought-stimulating experiences. If I don't feel like painting, I read something random or meet a stranger. It takes courage, but it works every time.

"New thoughts pop in that I can rabbit hole research, then I feel like painting again. I believe if I can keep my purpose alive and still be of value, I'll keep going. It's a consensus decision between me and the universe now."

Although every Hygge Queen's experience was unique, each allowed the power of fire and winds of hardship to shape her into a stronger, more refined human vessel. All relied to a greater or lesser extent on the following four affirmations.

Four Fire Affirmations:

1. *My fire turns every fear and obstacle to ash.*
2. *My inner flame sets the world ablaze and lights my way.*
3. *Passion, love, truth, and creativity spread like wildfire.*
4. *My spark of infinity is the immortal Me.*

CHAPTER 2

FIRE
POWER

*"You must be ready to burn yourself in your own flame;
how could you rise anew if you have not first become ashes?"*
– NIETZSCHE

When a canopy of loneliness arches over me, I like to revisit some of the world's harshest terrains. A strange solace lies in these vast uncompromising lands of shape and shadow. My soul can span dunes and saltpans, pause over pink flamingoes scooping beakfuls of brine shrimps. *Soar.*

The dry smack-in-the-face heat of the Atacama in South America echoes through my inner landscape, resonant with ancestral betrayal amid crumpled canyons, Valle de la Muerte, and blood-red rock crystals glinting in the setting sun.

On the northwest flank of Cerro Unita in the Tarapaca region is the 119-meter long Atacama Giant geoglyph depicting Tunupa, the god of volcano and lightning, whose task was to order the world. Tribes traded potent hallucinogens and sacrificed their children to Tunupa in this arid

105 000 km² area encompassing Chile's serpentine head, Bolivia, Peru, and Argentina.

Local Atacamians don scary masks, light fires, and perform death dances for tourists.

Today's Sacrificer needs no ax to ward off potential cataclysms: just a white coat or a clutch of press cards to persuade parents to deliver their children unto pharmaceutical Molochs.

What am I willing to sacrifice? Well, now, let's see. All my outdated identities, for a start. Harsh, perhaps, but necessary.

Their ball and chain sadness, propensity to cling to illusions, and wail at deaf gods in the sky that never reply have become tedious.

I'd rather be a volcano deity. I'd wallow in molten mutability, send purging lava to sear my slopes in fiery rivers of rage. Afterward, an upgrade and forging of new forms.

Pure elemental frequencies for all who choose earth's sovereignty. That would make me river, rock, cloud, and tree.

DESERT ORACLES

In the Sahara's Black Desert, iron pyrite remnants from volcanic eruptions spill across the sand. They resemble burnt toast crumbs.

As I totter up a dune slope, the wind accosts me like a Cairo street vendor, plucking at my clothes and ruffling my hair.

Something devastating happened in this barren, forsaken place. I'm sure of it.

Calcite and glittering quartz surround Crystal Mountain, a roofless cave heralding the start of the White Desert.

The hyperventilating Land Cruiser lurches on until golden limestone boulders and 50-meter-high inselbergs loom into view.

Winds over millennia have sculpted these silent sentinels into surrealistic shapes that lend the landscape a macabre beauty.

Embedded in the limestone walls are coral, mussel, and small conch shell fossils.

Our guide explains the entire Sahara was a pre-historic freshwater ocean, home to enormous sea creatures.

I ponder the legend of Tiamat and Abzu. The primordial Mesopotamian goddess, oft depicted as a giant dragon or sea serpent, mingled her salty ocean with Abzu's freshwater sea to bring the first gods into being.

Who was She? Did she create the cosmos? Did she make me?

Bedouin drums beat besides a skittering fire. A sense of emptiness as my being skims the Void like a bolide.

Few venture here. Bar the odd nomad, bowing only to Allah but tying up his camels all the same. A crescent moon and star twinkle against the night's celestial canopy.

Nuit, which means night in French, was the Egyptian sky goddess who swallowed the sun in the evening and birthed it again in the morning. Does my internal spark spin me through a life and death dance, steadying me at the crossover point of an infinity symbol between my temples?

If I'm part of the sun's energy, I'm also one with the Milky Way. Did the Great Mother lactate?

I stare up at the night sky. My star star(es) back at me. In the Afrikaans or Dutch vernacular, 'ster' anagrams to rest. Isn't that what the dead in heaven do?

Are we stardust? Does the word monster come from moon star? Maybe. Yet star appears in self-mastery, too. Is true mastery seeing through illusions?

Just as the sun will always outshine the moon, my atomic light will nullify all monsters eventually. At least, that's what I tell myself. The universe shares its limitless knowledge from inside me for free. It's a concept that comforts me.

In southern Africa's parched Transfrontier Kgalagadi, another mirage. After their shifts, the world's last remaining Bushmen exchange their loincloths for chinos and poison darts for cellphones. Seeing this, having spent the day with them learning to track wild animals, stash water in ostrich eggs, make friction fires, and darn with acacia thorns, made me sad. There was a time when the Kalahari San resonated to a different frequency.

Like all indigenous people on their landscape's wavelength, their connection with the Natural elements enabled them to traverse worlds using self-powering circuitry.

All humans could do this before something hijacked our attention. Some of us are waking up to it again.

FIRE WORKS

She's a white Afrikaans woman who keeps the Khoi San tradition alive. Liesl Haasbroek, an elementor, teaches this primal friction fire skill.

The visceral joy South Africa's foremost fire queen brings to her workshops mesmerizes all who watch and participate.

The magic begins with gathering the kindling, a feminine woodpile collaboration of dried fynbos and Protea seed heads.

There's extra sand on hand "if the fire spirits become too happy."

The enthralled Khoi descendants in her audience watch how the slim barefoot Prometheus sparks embers to the rhythmic beat of a didgeridoo using a bow and a hard masculine Mozambique kiaat stick to generate heat with the motherboard.

Her twin flame Dr. Bruce Copley, the first to resurrect this lost art, keeps the rhythm going. The earth and air seem to hold their breath as Liesl summons the first element in a moment, a lifetime. An ember sparks a dried flower; a flame crackles into culmination – silence bursts into applause. My internal fire rejoices.

Fierce as a raging inferno one minute; gentle as a flowing stream the next, many would call Ms. Haasbroek one badass woman. She prefers the word Elementor.

Her primal connection with Nature inspires all who hire her to create ceremonial fires for weddings, birthdays, funerals, ancestral and community gatherings.

An astrologer specializing in life purpose charts told Liesl she was born to this transformative calling, but it took her a few years to realize this for herself.

"The astrologist said I would become a 'sacred divine magician.' I rolled my eyes but recalled her words just the other day while explaining to children how the magic tricks you see on television are all lies and illusions.

"The real magic is to generate fires with Nature's elements. The fire generated by the heart and fueled by the sun runs our bodies, making us all Fire Queens and Kings.

"I worked in biodynamic agriculture for years, so I always appreciated the elemental connections. Nothing operates in isolation.

"The elements are in us. "Once we learn to use them as purification tools, we come into our power. Fire is potent when it manifests as enthusiastic energy. The fire of conviction can purify the fire of addiction."

TOXIC LEGACIES

The leaves of our family trees curl in the presence of flames. Northern European people sing and dance around a midsummer bonfire to spark bonhomie and ward off residual hearts of darkness.

Some two-legged beings are less human than others, animated – it would seem – by an alien frequency devoid of love. They resemble us physically, but their indifferent cruelty unveils them as they strike with speed and precision.

That's why treacherous people get called snakes, but what if there's more to it than that?

Is it so far-fetched to wonder about a possible reptile human genetic merge when so many Scandinavian statues depict precisely that, at least to my eye?

Oslo's Vigeland Park has humans struggling with giant lizard statues. Rudolph Tegner's Hercules and the Hydra sculpture outside Hamlet's 16th-century castle in Helsingør is another example. David Icke's hypothesis of reptile control among the elite is a global counter-cultural trend that continues to captivate millions.[1]

European reptile statues notwithstanding, I can neither prove nor disprove his theory, but some tales of aristocratic cruelty speak of cold-bloodedness to the extreme.

At Denmark's Dragsholm castle northwest of Zealand, 1910 structural renovations uncovered Celestine de Bayonne Guildenstern's skeleton. Her father had her bricked up alive inside the wall. What prompted

---

1   Kahn, 2005

this heinous act? A guide told us she fell pregnant at 16 by a stable hand when she'd been promised to a nobleman.

Celestine remains in situ, still wearing a dirty white dress, her jaw frozen in a petrified scream.

James Hepburn – Scotland's 4th Earl of Bothwell and third husband of Mary Queen of Scots – was chained to a pillar here for 10 years. Deep, circular grooves in the floor dug from his constant foot shuffling remain.

All the while, guests ate saddle of venison, drank wine, danced, and courted at the Great Hall's royal parties, weddings, and balls. And, if they heard a half-smothered wail from behind the wall, it "interrupted neither the cheerful laughter nor the tender kisses," wrote Jens Munk.[2]

Dragholm's uneven walls now house a boutique hotel and Michelin-starred restaurant. Sleep eluded me the night I stayed there, even though I had liberally availed myself of the wines.

Dread dogged my thoughts in the wee hours. The bathroom light kept switching on, repeatedly shining for minutes, then dark again. Celestine's ghost? Other daughters betrayed by their fathers, kickstarting a sense of emptiness?

SLOW-BURNING BETRAYALS

When an accountant weighs his daughter's worth in terms of expenditure, she will feel surplus to requirements. Alexandra's father drew up a diagram of his assets and liabilities to show her precisely what she had cost him financially over the years.

He listed her first in the liabilities column.

"He never wanted children. A need for financial security drove him because he lost his father in the war. I never felt loved or even worthy of love, empty inside.

"This disconnection from my true Self dragged me down a dark path. I compromised and negated myself at every level.

"I supported my partner to try and prove my financial worth.

"I even let him persuade me to terminate our pregnancy. He threatened to leave if I didn't.

---

2   History Scotland, 2019

"He left me anyway and had a baby with another woman a few months later. I was attacked and beaten in my home, to top it all off. The smacks from the universe kept getting harder and harder."

"I'd been having tremendous stomach pain. The doctors dismissed it as IBS, so it was almost a relief when the eventual diagnosis of stomach cancer came.

"Emergency surgery removed the tumor, leaving me with 100 stitches. While still on morphine after the operation, I had a vivid hallucination. The grey-robed Grim Reaper carrying his scythe in the periphery of my vision said he'd come to collect me.

"Three angels on my other side indicated a forked path. They said it was up to me to choose life or death. I took the way of life.

"Some soul searching helped me realize I had brought my misfortune on myself by allowing men to rob me of my self-esteem, wisdom, and usefulness.

"Cancer, the loss of my aborted baby, my boyfriend's abandonment of me, the attack in my home were events pushing me towards my best life. Now it's the one I keep choosing."

Alexandra lives in the country with a younger man who adores her. She spends most of her time rescuing animals, healing wild birds, and working with horses.

It's not just fathers who betray their daughters. Mothers can be equally guilty.

Madeleine's mother attracted men like moths to a flame with her striking looks and red mane. Her voice was low, her flirtatiously arched eyebrows matched a merry laugh. Madeleine alone knew her mother was a wicked witch, her beauty the artful application of cosmetics and wigs.

She always put men before Madeleine and blamed her when they fled her unchecked insanity. No bogeyman or monster in the cupboard held any fears for young Madeleine.

Her mother was scarier than the worst of them. She'd beat her with wooden spoons, a belt, or whatever came to hand.

"Scram, you ungrateful little bitch before I kill you," she would scream. Madeleine learned to flinch at sudden movements.

Recurring falling dreams shook her awake just before she hit the ground. At 18, she overdosed on pills. Her suicide attempt was a turning point.

"I entered a dream-like realm where I understood I could plunge further down my dark well of grief or heal a long line of abuse instead.

"My falling dreams felt like my spirit descending into matter. Nobody was coming to rescue me. I would have to show up for myself.

"Trite as it sounds, I felt like Cinderella receiving her fairy godmother's magic wand. There was power in knowing everything was up to me. The more I worked on emotional independence from my mother, the stronger I became.

Leaving home, marrying, divorcing, having a daughter of my own were all bricks in the four-decade, winding road I'm still walking towards my Self."

Raised by a cruel woman, Mel Gouws was relieved to discover she and her sister were adopted.

"You can't choose family, they say. But my family picked me from a lineup, so they did choose me. They said they found me under a gooseberry bush. I spent hours under the gooseberry bush in the garden as a child, longing to be elsewhere.

"My mother loved to parade my sister (adopted from a different Mum) and me in front of visitors, making us sing or play the piano.

"We had to train for endless ballet and music eisteddfods. On the nightmarish drive home, she would lambast us for mistakes.

"My sweet Dad was physically and mentally ill. Mum would not accept help nursing him. She sent us to boarding school instead.

"Fuelled by subconscious abandonment issues, I was an angry, rebellious teen. I got expelled. Mum never forgave me.

"My sister and I discovered our adoption quite accidentally in our late teens, much to Mum's mortification. I was delighted.

"That was the day I found myself. Finally, things made sense.

"I did not share DNA with this cruel woman who hissed at us behind closed doors: 'You came from the gutter, and that's where you're going.'

"Mum set about destroying the intense bond between my sister and me. She estranged us for ten years, but we put the pieces together after she died.

"As we helped each other heal, we made a pact to give each other the unwavering, unconditional love we'd never had.

"Now we have a beautiful relationship, no matter what. Love survived, despite Mum."

Christine Ann Lawson writes in *Understanding The Borderline Mother* that small children cannot discern between their mother's beliefs and their own. They understand neither deception nor incongruence that "mother might feel one emotion while expressing another or that hostility may be masked with a smile."[3]

Christina Crawford, the adoptive daughter of the famous actress Joan, describes her childhood as "an abyss, a black hole, a juggernaut of chaos (where) fabrication, anger, and turmoil reigned supreme. (A place of) no help, no peace, and no escape."[4]

Bronwyn was doubly betrayed by her mother when she plucked up the courage to tell her that her older brother had abused her when they were growing up.

"She called me wicked for accusing my saintly brother of such a heinous crime and promptly cut me out of her will. She died four months afterward, and my brother got everything.

"It left a bitter taste, especially as I struggle financially and he lives the life of Riley, but I had to move on.

"What else could I do? I can't change what happened. I know whatever festers inside me will only make me ill. Sometimes the high road is the only way."

Total estrangement is how Lynn handled the aftermath of an abusive childhood. "I had to cut my mother loose to save my sanity. I have not spoken to her in 30 years and have no regrets. Nothing I did was ever good enough for her. "No matter how much I tried to please her, she made me feel shameful and wrong.

"Her toxic mood swings drained my energy. Yet, she loved to paint herself as the victim.

---

3   Lawson, 2004
4   Crawford, 2018

"I cut ties after I overheard her badmouthing me to my children. She tried to turn them against me. "A family feels less about biology and more about loving acceptance to me now," she says.

FIERY FOREBEARS

You come from a long line of lunatics. *Rude!* I know. Sorry. It's true, though. And thank goodness because we need a little madness to shake things up.

You wouldn't be here if not for the crazy schemes of your forebears. You're here because of their courage, insanity, pain, and perseverance. They will always live inside you, but you can throw off the mantle of their beliefs that no longer apply.

Think of yourself as the ancestor rewriting your family's cellular pattern. Zanna helps her clients address familial beliefs in their lineage to move forward.

"You can face the legacy of a core wound, let go of the inherited beliefs around painful stories and release the trauma for everyone," she says.

"But there's more to transmuting a situation than simply changing your thoughts.

"We can only facilitate change in ourselves once we acknowledge what our ancestors did to survive. Even if it seems dysfunctional or inapplicable to these times, they did it to protect us, the realization of their dreams. We repeat the same patterns in different settings because our bodies hold their memories. For example, Bev was always in a hurry and never made enough time for herself.

We uncovered that her father constantly reprimanded her for 'wasting time on nothing.'

"He and her paternal grandparents were industry workers in a competitive market. The faster they got the job done, the more they got paid. Dashing about helped them succeed.

"Once Bev thanked her ancestors for their hard work and surrendered their beliefs to a candle flame, she overcame her sense of urgency and found ample time to do as she pleased.

"Your ancestry is here to protect you," says Zanna. "They live in your body and perpetuate those patterns for your safety. Honor, rather than worship, is appropriate.

"Thank them and respectfully acknowledge their choices before declaring your intent to release patterns that no longer serve you. It's a gentle way to transmit energy and effect positive change through conscious awareness.

"Inner ancestral work is a way to communicate and interact with your body cells.

"When I became aware of a maternal fear pattern holding me back, I lit a candle, tuned in to the aspects of my mother I had to release, and made my feelings known.

"The subtle shift I felt inside enabled me to let go and thrive. I love the notion that I am my ancestors' dream come true."

Likewise, when Madeleine burned the deadwood of her mother's cruel compulsions – "a recurring loveless childhood motif" interlaced down her maternal line – the misery-addicted versions of herself dissipated in smoke.

"I could have banged that abusive Mother drum for longer, but it was only hurting me. Inwardly razing memories and fearful, compliant versions of myself set me free," she says.

TRANSFORMATION CONFLAGRATION

Your relationship with the fire element can rearrange reality, says Jacqueline.

While healing happens when you acknowledge, face, and transmute a familial pattern, without a good connection with the fire element, she warns you could surrender passion for falsity and drown in the waters of your ancestral line. Just as healing something in yourself can heal your entire lineage, your personal decisions affect thousands of others in your reality.

"The real bombshell, the big happening," she says, "is that you can rearrange reality by not complying with anything that doesn't feel right for you.

"Tens of thousands, hundreds of thousands stop complying when you do. You control reality."

Your divine atomic spark is part of an interconnective gold frequency that animates everything. In a "two-way switch" process not unlike the internet, it collects and floods the multidimensional universe with information about you. Anything that doesn't resonate with Pure Love's gold frequency comes from a "slave-self setting."

Jacqueline says these identities continue to suffer rejection, pain, and other unpleasant reflections as long as you let them stay. "As soon as you allow the heat of your inner suns to reduce those problem personalities to ash, you find whatever you need to heal in a flash.

"It might be an encounter with someone or a connection with a voice in your head."[5]

Flames of hope

Dr. Christiane Northrup's inner voice responded right away when she fell to her knees and silently called for help.

Named in 2021 by *Watkins Magazine* as one of the 100 Most Spiritually Influential Living People, Dr. Northrup shares on a podcast with Jacqueline how she overruled a prognosis of 'inevitable' blindness pronounced by doctors at a world-renowned clinic.

When a clouded cornea in her left eye festered, she secured a corneal biopsy with the head of the Cornea Unit at the Massachusetts Eye and Ear Infirmary.

"Believe me; you never want one of those," she says.

Slides confirmed the ophthalmologist's initial diagnosis of Infectious Crystalline Keratopathy. Only 70 cases of this rare condition afflicting immunocompromised people exist in world literature.

"He put me on hourly high-power antibiotics in the infirmary.

"The disruption of being forced awake every hour to ingest them sent my cortisol levels rocketing. Sleep is the most effective way to digest stress hormones, and I wasn't getting any."

---

5   Oraclegirl.org Track of the Month 4, December 13, 2021

When she raised her concerns, the doctor told her to persevere with the regime since germs grew 24/7.

The blindness in her left eye worsened.

"I thought ... this is never going to get better. And I wasn't getting better. I knew I couldn't heal in such an unruly environment."

On the fourth day, Dr. Northrup fell to her knees and silently implored: Help me, please!"

At once, she remembered. Vitamin C. Of course! She got onto it right away.

"I have an iron-clad stomach, so I took 50 grams of Vitamin C a day in divided doses. My cornea cleared up after the first massive dose."

Dr. Northrup is glad she only read about Infectious Crystalline Keratopathy's grim prognosis and the 70 known cases after restoring her sight. "I didn't go blind because I didn't know it was the only known option," she says.

"Googling a medical condition can implant a belief system more firmly in your biology. I wouldn't recommend it to anyone. Had I learned about the inevitable blindness associated with my condition too soon, I might have thought all was lost.

"My colleague Bruce Lipton wrote a book called *Biology of Belief* – and that's where we are right now. (There is) the desperate need to change the belief to what is possible.

"We are so much stronger than we think so long as we don't give our beliefs away to a system more invested in profits than cures," she says. "I'd love everyone to know our Self Healing Ability – something we've had from the beginning – is always available."[6]

The currency among those tuned into their self-healing abilities is a healthy interdependence rather than a *quid pro quo* or monetary-based system, even though these concepts may apply.

The days of working on yourself and "making things happen" through methods and formulae are over. These are slave-self misconceptions. Jacqueline says rituals can be worthy in their rightful place, but you never have to go outside yourself for anything.

---

6   Northrup, 2021

Just as active volcanos might represent an external purification of your slave-self settings, burning can facilitate the transmutation of grief and fear.

Fire is a metaphor for truth. Stand on your head if you like, but it's all a matter of frequency. Either you resonate at the level of your inner suns – Jacqueline says we have *two* – or the pathway of possibility connecting the collective and individual human existence is closed to you.

"It's about you materializing (anything) using your source connection," says Jacqueline. "In the company of others on that golden frequency level, you switch into that pure love resonance. You automatically generate self-healing abilities to dissolve undesirable circumstances or send the perfect person to help you with a problem. "You can rearrange reality now, quickly because you control reality. (This) is the bombshell, the big happening."[7]

Sound of sunshine

The Sun (plays) a secret melody hidden inside itself that produces a widespread throbbing motion of its surface.
– Kenneth R. Lang

The Sun predates Yahweh and all religions. First entity in the Void, progenitor of all life and matter, we human beings are solar entities, suns, and sons of our creator.

The *Sun Book* was the first Egyptian papyrus edition of ancient stone-transcribed astrotheological observations that gave rise to the Helio, or Holy Judeo-Christian Bible – from Byblos, the Phoenician City of the Great Mother.[8]

The Sun guides you in and out of life by first purifying and then flipping into a materialization effect.

As Jacqueline puts it: "The sun aspect of you resonates on the gold frequency that opens the doorway to the entire universe.

---

7   Oraclegirl.org., Your Self Healing Abilities with Dr. Northrup, Sept 17 2021
8   Spaceagebachelor, 2007

"This most potent, transmutative aspect of the Sun's corona or plasmic aura of our being, the glow of our material presence, and the manifestation of pure love in this world" is the reason for sun worship since the dawn of humankind.[9]

Before 1945, doctors prescribed sunlight to heal every condition, from tuberculosis to festering wounds. However, sun prophylactics and antibiotics generated more profitable returns than natural healing; solar demonization soon followed.

The industrial negation of sunshine defies logic since humans are diurnal. If the Sun were harmful, we would have died out long ago. Our bodies are like batteries.

We need sunlight to recharge. Without it, we get stressed and anxious.

Most commercial sunscreens include Oxybenzone or Benzophenone-3, Avobenzone, Homosalate, Octinoxate (Octylmethoxycinnamate), Cylcopentasiloxane or Cyclomethicone, Phthalates, Parabens.[10]

These hormone disruptors can cause endometriosis, cancers, metabolic diseases, neurological disabilities, cardiac and respiratory problems. In May 2021, the FDA recalled 78 brands of sunscreens over carcinogen contamination.[11]

Sunglasses, another 20th-century invention, became high-fashion items 'to cry behind,' according to a popular 60s song.

Also, they block essential signaling for calcium and melanin stimulated by the Sun's biophotons to enter the eyes.

Florida neurosurgeon Dr. Jack Kruse says sunglasses create hypoxia in retinas and photoreceptor damage.

ROS/RNS (reactive oxygen species that damage cells, causing reactive nitrosative stress) increase.[12]

We trust our gut feeling, but who knew gut bacteria also generated electricity?

---

9   Oraclegirl.org Library Track of the Month 4, 2022
10 Shannon, 2019
11 Cara, 2021
12 Kruse, 2020

New research from the University of California, Berkeley, shows that bacteria in the human gut, from pathogenic to probiotic, are electrogenic.[13]

Our digestion itself s a process of electrical fermentation (Air) and combustion. (Fire)

Seven ways the sun restores your energy

1. *The Sun sings all the time. A complex pattern of acoustic waves coursing through its interior causes it to vibrate. Birds sing to the beat of these rhythmic sounds that Nasa has recorded. Bees dance, and happy bees hum in the key of C, not B. Who knew?*
2. *Sunlight's ultrasound frequency kills bacteria in seconds.*
3. *Promotes hormonal production: A Boston State Hospital study saw a testosterone increase of 120% in men exposed to UV light on their chests and backs.*
4. *Sunlight UVA creates Vitamin D3, a neurosteroid essential for immune function, cell growth control, and curbing many cancers. Unpasteurized milk, butter, and eggs contain D3, but raw dairy products are illegal in many European countries. and American states. Catch 22. High-fructose corn syrup in processed food blocks Vitamin D absorption.*
5. *The Sun emits 'light codes' that energize and awaken you to your divine golden frequency. A few rays outside help you bounce back from burnout from the havoc artificial lighting and LED devices inflict on your circadian rhythms.*
6. *Convert sunlight into joy by speaking your intentions to the sunrise. Do this barefoot on the beach, grass, or ground for faster results*
7. *Name and release whatever you don't want into the sunset. Dawn and dusk are the only times you can safely look at the Sun.*

---

13   Portnoy, 2018

PURIFYING FIRE RITUALS

Fire ceremonies are recreational, creative, and healing. Make yours as simple or complex as you like, says Liesl Haasbroek, but never light candles near open windows, curtains, or electronics, as melting wax can run everywhere.

"Rituals are better performed outdoors unless you have a proper indoor fireplace. Flames jump and dance, so ensure you always have a large pot of sand at hand.

"Be clear about what emotional and mental concepts you'd like to burn. Frame questions differently. Reflect on what you can learn from something that upset you rather than asking why it happened. Think about everything you'd like to release.

"Write or depict negative thoughts, situations, or triggering letters you want to purge and transform. The swift disintegration of rolling papers or Rizlas makes a great visual metaphor.

"Light a candle before you have a courageous conversation.

"You can curate the kindling with soft feminine and hard masculine woods for maximum collaboration. I love fragrant woods and dried seed heads for a flower fire that engages the senses of smell and hearing."

Friction, explains Liesl, is more potent than sheer strength.

"You do not make fire with force. You use rhythm. I like the friction method for ceremonial burning because it takes effort and focus. Some blow the ember into flame to symbolize the contribution of their life force.

"The transformative potency of a primal fire can connect you with your ancestors' energy.

"You can sit quietly by the fire and contemplate the talents and traumatic tales that constitute your familial topography.

"What traits do you share with siblings or cousins? Do you recognize the trigger pattern from your familial past? With patience, you can uncover and extinguish underlying thoughts such as 'I am not valuable' that feed fears or bad memories.

"The next step is to build new habits and ethical pathways to override future triggers.

It takes a little discipline, but you can ask your healed ancestors for guidance, courage, inspiration, and renewed vitality.

"You can reset your life with the respectful acknowledgment, integration, and healing of a core familial wound that liberates everyone through time.

"You change patterns by making better choices. Generational pain that ends with you heals the entire collective. Resistance brings struggle, but the process never has to be painful. Ease, kindness, feminine softness, and vulnerability remove ancestral blockages more effectively.

"A good cry can be cathartic. When healing tears get shed, I burn the used tissues, too.

"I like to introduce ritual and ceremony to our children. Not just for their birthdays, but also if they feel sad.

"If something upsetting happened at school, let your child draw or write it privately. Then burn it together.

"The transformative power of one element becoming another is accessible to everyone."

Scottish artist Caroline Morris says Gary M Douglas and Dr. Dain Heer's Access Consciousness tools helped her.[14]

"When I require clarity, I ask what my life will be like in five or 20 years if I choose whatever I'm considering. Does a prospect make me feel expansive or heavy? My inner flame tells me.

"My body always knows what's true. If something feels too heavy, I like to ask myself what else is possible. What would it take for everything to work out better than I ever imagined?

"We are a frequency of golden light sparkling through everything, and we can make it fun."

Shamama Artio, artist and ordained Priestess of the Sacred Feminine, has two outdoor fire pits in her oceanside community in Gualala, Northern California.

I do all of my fire purification work outdoors to be safe. When troubled, I sit and gaze at the fire until my mind finds a peaceful resolution. I give thanks for my life and say a prayer for anyone needing comfort.

---

14   Douglas, 2021

"Afterward, you can sprinkle water you've blessed or rose petals over the ashes before adding them to a compost heap or scatter them in the wind. Do whatever feels right for you."

CANDLE RITUALS

Nkogono Mantsielo, a Johannesburg-based *umthandazi* or traditional healer and prophet, says candle wax represents a tree trunk's stability and strength. It reminds you to keep your intentions grounded with your Earth connection.

As the flame dances with the air and the wax melts, the candle's form changes from solid to liquid.

"This connects us to water and our emotional desires. The melting candle symbolizes the merging of four elements into a fifth – spirit or aether."

Lesedi candle smoke portents

AN ABUNDANCE OF SMOKE: *The air element invites you to parse out your thoughts and look at the bigger picture for a greater understanding.*

SMOKE THAT DRIFTS AWAY FROM YOU: *Dissipating energy diffuses your purpose. If your ritual is for another's benefit, drifting smoke indicates the desired effect of your intent.*

SMOKE THAT MOVES TOWARD YOU: *A positive outcome and the granting of your request. Also, an indication of unintended consequences if your intentions are hostile.*

WHITE SMOKE: *A positive sign that indicates the granting of your request, especially if it appears as you contemplate your desire.*

BLACK SMOKE: *The candle says no. Somebody or something is in the way. Negative energies work against you. You may need to do more self-purification before attempting this ritual again.*

How to read a flame

STRONG: *An excellent portent. Your intentions worked. You will receive the outcome you desire.*

WEAK: *Negative influences resist you.*

DANCING: *Expect raw emotions and explosions of energy.*

TWISTING: *False friends and deception.*

EXTINGUISHED: *Abandon the project for now. You may need to put in more work or energy.*

DIRECTION: *If the flame moves north, something physical is manifesting. South is a sign of a new love relationship, east is all about new ideas, and west portends success.*

Source: Nkogono Mantsielo

Quick Fixes

MAKE SUNSCREEN AT HOME:
Mix zinc powder into a handful of face cream or body lotion, apply, and you're good to go.

SMUDGE NEGATIVE ENERGY:
Burn dried herbs for spiritual cleansing. Sage, dried lavender, and Impepho smoke all work well.
Visualize everything you'd like to clear, light your smudge bundle, and watch the swirling smoke disperse into the atmosphere.

CHAPTER 3

FIRE QUEEN

"Sky in our lungs, land beneath our feet, fire in our soul, and water in our blood."
– Emily R. King, The Fire Queen

Like many, I began to wake up during the lockdown. Stuff I once cared about – a picture byline in a national newspaper, say – lay in tatters around my feet. I know. *Cringe*

That was before my ghosts dissipated like smoke from the bonfire of then. Pretentious? *Moi?* Bongwater for tea held more appeal than the pandemic skullduggery.

Masked men conjure memories of perverts with poor bin-balancing skills. I encountered such a creep – a bandana covering his lower face – at my bedroom window. Cue startled shrieks, clattering metal lids, and cats fleeing the alley below. It was long ago, but even so.

The word mask now dominates our social lexicon like never before. Everything is masked, including the truth, whatever that is.

At least, masked balls popular among the Italian aristocracy might have provided a modicum of romantic intrigue. I drift into a frowsy furbe-low of Venetian daydreams – colorful papier-mâché carnival masks, pick-pockets, and pigeons on San Marco Square. A decaying archipelago of an aesthetic past, where once – "Your nose is showing."

What? A man in the supermarket interrupts my reverie. Belly quiver-ing behind straining shirt buttons, he pokes my chest with a fat forefin-ger. "Cover your nose."

"Don't touch me," I hiss. Heart thumping, I abandon my trolley and skedaddle.

Back in my garden, embraced by the warm sunshine, I took stock. Order online from here?

Good idea. My latent agoraphobic self agreed.

I'd morphed from globe trotter to self-isolating hermit.

People were beginning to frighten the bejeezus out of me. Mothers muzzled toddlers in prams.

Neighbors clanged pots at the moon. Nurses bopped between bed-pans and gyrated around drip stands on TikTok videos. That puzzled me the most.

Wasn't much call for choreography when I was a nurse. Shirking – nev-er mind twerking to *Big, Big Bootie*, or *Swing to the Jab* – was discouraged.

I had no idea who I was supposed to be in this bamboozling Blade Runner meets *The Matrix* tetralogy. Nothing made sense.

Bootleggers boogied to alcohol-and-cigarette bans in South Africa, where police turned water cannons on disabled grant recipients.

Restaurants closed. Unemployment figures rocketed.

And still, people continued to parrot official narratives on social media. Fawning devotees praised a president whose government goons arrested beach walkers, tore children from their parents' arms, and shot dead an Alex township dweller for a case of beer.

Roast chicken, open-toed sandals, and women's underwear joined a puzzling list of contraband sales.

Contradicting the long-established scientific herd immunity defini-tion – enough people acquiring natural resistance to infectious disease

– the WHO stated only vaccinations could achieve it in 2020.[1] The CDC changed its 'producing immunity' vaccination definition to 'producing protection' in September 2021.[2]

A PREDATORY PANDEMIC

Recycling became the new religion, even as disposable masks cause unprecedented environmental damage, with 451,500 tons of toxic medical trash dumped into oceans, rivers, and landfills every month.[3]

Hand sanitizer replaced holy water in the cult of cognitive dissonance, a steaming fusion of religion and spirituality. Poverty became the new penitence.

As priests and gurus fell from grace, corporate rule replaced god. At least, it did its damnedest.

Water treaders in heaving seas – not waving so much as virtue-signaling – watched in dismay as their livelihoods sank.

"Fully vaxxed" – whatever that means in these days of boosters and vaccine passports – festooned social media profiles with homespun homilies and a call to arms.

Some proclaimed a 'healthy distrust of authority but took the jab anyway.'

Wait. A healthy distrust of authority, you say? Riiight.

"Stay safe" is still the annoying buzzword *du jour*.

"I've had my shot; you're welcome," or "Let's get vaccinated" became the new enticement as though we were now shelter dogs.

Not me. My shots involved tequila, salt, and a slice of lemon as a rapid restorative. Facebook's unfriend button worked overtime.

Those who chose to wait for verified safety-test results – dubbed 'refuseniks' or 'vax hesitant' by the media – were uninvited to weddings and other social functions.

Significant savings on gifts aside, nobody could explain why their vaccines did not protect them. They could not see through *their* spectacles

---

1   Margolis, 2021
2   Mercola, 2021
3   Edwards, 2021

if you did not wear yours, went the argument; might poop in their pants unless *you* wore a diaper.

While many recovered from Covid, others succumbed to heart issues and cancer.

"A short illness" became the media euphemism for people dying unexpectedly within months of a second jab. Sudden cardiac deaths among FIFA athletes increased 5-fold in 2021.[4]

Enthralled government leaders and corporates bombarded citizens with sugary incentives. Some brothels even offered free sex for jabbed clients.[5]

Wasn't that female exploitation? Where were the virtue signallers now? The irony seemed lost on most.

If enticements failed to work, threats followed. Using public transport or shopping at supermarkets were among the rights snatched from the unjabbed.

Australian authorities forbade refuseniks in the Northern Territories to leave their homes for any reason, detained, then deported the world's No. 1 tennis player Novak Djokovic, rather than risk making him "an icon of free choice."[6]

Even after Pfizer CEO Albert Bourla admitted the first two doses and booster offered "very little if any" protection, countries like Austria imposed fines of up to €3,600 on its unvaxxed citizens.[7] [8]

Yet, public compliance and approval of restrictive two-tiered, Apartheid societies continued apace.

Life felt like a Jim Jones revival competition to see who could gulp the Kool-Aid fastest. Many held out their mugs for more as the narrative fluctuated from month to month.

Western media outlets promoted videos and images to show people in Wuhan dropping or lying dead in the streets. Most of this footage turned out to be fake.[9]

---

4   Sones, 2021
5   Cailler, 2021
6   David, 2022
7   RiseMelbourne, 2022
8   L.P., 2022
9   Swiss Policy Research, 2022

You could test positive for Covid with no symptoms whatsoever. People swallowed that chestnut so fast I thought of *The Naked Emperor*. How only the unbrainwashed – an innocent child – could see through the ruse. Was Hans Christian Andersen hinting at hypnosis or *Mass Formation Psychosis*, a condition for totalitarianism, even then?

The lugubrious Danish author wrote some ripping yarns, but his all-consuming attractions to non-reciprocal men predisposed him to melancholy. Doubtless, he would have masked up alone in a rape field or whatever they grew then.

Anyone who seeks emotional nourishment outside of themselves will continue to experience all manner of non-reciprocal relationships – just saying.

I encountered non-reciprocal men, women, colleagues, friends, and even family members on my sovereign path. Was I alone detecting subtle, indefinable changes in many of them?

In the dawning light of comprehension, I began to perceive things I could not unsee. Their lack of empathy, inability to comfort, and constant parroting of corporate narratives sucked the loosh out of me. Something cold, machine-like, and predatory drove their behavior. Their responses seemed Pavlovian, their reactions robotic. Had they always been devoid of discernible emotional literacy, adept at mimicry? They felt more humanoid than human – everything was their way or the highway.

Talking heads on the TV sounded like androids under remote control. Former colleagues now felt like total strangers to me. Inwardly, I dubbed them 'replicants' for doggedly sticking to insane narratives urging me to say 'yes' when my entire being screamed 'oh, hell to the no!'

Every dream came with a soundtrack and a prepackaged batch of spirituality. "It is what it is. Love and light, darlings! Tomorrow is another day. You don't say!"

Was I starring in a personalized Truman Show-type soap opera?

Shakespeare said the world was a stage, but global community theatre felt more accurate. The first man to receive the Pfizer vaccine was William Shakespeare from Warwickshire, who died five months later after a stroke.[10]

---

10   Fuller, 2021

Novak's detention – no vax – sounds like a djoke. The BBC reporter covering petrol shortages was called Phil McCann.[11]

REEL LIFE

Now, World War 3 looms with the usual villain of the piece – as though everything rests on the shoulders of one man. Popular prejudice favors the neighboring country's president, another actor whose TV appearances include dancing bare-chested in stiletto heels[12] and playing the piano with his penis.[13]

Many of the faithful have exchanged their social media pro-jab frames for the yellow and blue hues of that country's flag, vehemently attacking anyone who holds an opposing opinion. I wish I were making this up, but who would believe you even if you fictionalized this?

So much of what I knew came from Tell-lie-vision – proud purveyors of CGI and Hollywood trickery.

Everything I'd once thought real turned out to be fake, from cultural figures to the shape of our Earth – not so much flat as a crater, I reckon. Either way, I doubt it's the spinning ball they say.

"You sew the world into a globe with a thread about how Columbus thought America was India," says author James True.[14]

The researcher, Wim Godgevlamste, lays out compelling evidence on his YouTube channel to show an Antarctic ice wall surrounding our Sulpicius Gallus M crater reflected from our Plasma moon.[15]

There are no heroes on the world stage – only actors. Names listed on the Internet Movie Database (IMDb) include Neil Armstrong (first man on the moon), Neil "pear-shaped earth" deGrasse Tyson, Bill Gates, Joe Rogan (alternative media truther), and Novak Djokovic (world-class tennis player).[16]

---

11   Euro Journal, 2021

12   Ramkat, 2022

13   @KyleTrouble, 2022

14   True, 2022

15   godgevlamste, 2020

16   IMDb, n.d.

As Vladimir Lenin said: "The best way to control the opposition is to lead it ourselves."

In well-researched essays, artist-scientist Miles W Mathis pulls apart numerous mainstream narratives to show lifetime actors play iconic roles to perpetuate cultural agendas.

"Every famous person I have researched so far has been part of some hoax, so now I assume almost every famous person who died early or mysteriously has faked it.

"That should also be your default assumption. If (the mainstream media) tell you it is day, assume it is night," he wrote in his paper on Elvis Presley.

Twins Aron and Elvis played the Rock n Roll King role. Aron married Priscilla and went into the army, while Elvis made records and dallied with Ann Margret. Neither twin died in 1977.[17]

Mathis includes John Lennon, Marilyn Monroe, The Kennedys, Jim Morrison, Janis Joplin, Sharon Tate, Jimi Hendrix, Jack London, River Phoenix, Tupac Shakur, Kurt Cobain, James Dean, Paul Walker, Robin Williams, John Belushi, Natalie Wood, William Holden, Chris Kyle, George Reeves, Nicole Simpson, Brittany Murphy, Bruce Lee, Grace Kelly, Princess Diana, Michael Jackson, Heath Ledger, and many more in his impressive body of work.

Today stock phrases such as "I Can't Breathe" are rinsed and recycled into all sorts of one-size-fits-all occasions.

Eric Garner, murdered in 2014 by a New York policeman, said it first. On May 25, 2020, George Floyd repeated it at the knee of Minneapolis police officer Derek Chauvin choking him.

"I Can't Breathe" reverberated in Black Lives Matter protests worldwide.[18]

"I Can't Breathe." Dozens screamed the phrase at Travis Scott's Astroworld Festival in Houston that killed eight and injured hundreds on November 5, 2021.[19]

---

17   Mathis, 2015
18   Wikipedia, n.d.
19   Newstead, 2021

Now climate change activists are repurposing the phrase for air pollution and environmental issues.[20]

Scramble the letters and "I Can't Breathe" anagrams into "A Better China." Coincidence?

Increasingly, 'reel life' felt more like a one-fits-all construct meted out to "slaves born into bondage," as Morpheus told Neo in *The Matrix*. Hollywood embeds the truth for those with ears to hear and "real eyes to realize."

Ironically people had to use their QR codes on their vaccine passports to see *Matrix 4* in a cinema. In December 2021, Parisian police stormed the cinema interrupting the movie to inspect audience IDs. Talk about blue-pilled![21]

By February 2022, 'two weeks to flatten the curve' 2020's rhetoric had segued into "mass testing for HIV" and frozen bank accounts of any Canadian who donated $25 to the trucking convoy.[22]

New Zealanders faced arrest and seizure of their property for refusing Covid tests.[23]

People succumbed to heart attacks, cancers, and suicide. Zoom funerals became a thing. Stringent conditions to go shopping, cruising, or even places of worship – demanded approved pharmaceutical IDs.

The widening void between choices seemed like a deliberate fostering of friction. Diversity had become uniformity.

Propaganda and "pharmacologically-enhanced brainwashing" enthralled people to the nth degree. Many seemed to relish losing their liberty to coercion and conformity.

Something had switched down my capacity and hijacked my reality with the intent of enslavement. Whichever of my Bewildered Betty identities had consented to this would have to burn on a funeral pyre of Old Me's. And sharpish!

What if we weren't just aging meat suits but divine technology – dream machines capable of shaking "them" off like fleas?

---

20 Chow, 2020
21 VigilantFox, 2021
22 @canadianaco, 2022
23 @libsoftiktok, 2022

What if they needed us to manifest their dark desires, provide flesh vehicles to do their bidding, and live on the Earth's surface?

Genetic blending for more control? They knew we wouldn't surrender in the full knowledge of our innate divinity.

They'd have to distract us with songs, programs, and disinformation from birth. That way, few of us would realize our worth. Things sure looked that way, but who were "they?"

Progeny of Yaldabaoth, the Demiurge? Gnostic Archons? Reptilians? An ancient A.I. Hivemind? Knights of Ni?

What if some Lovecraftian Cthulhu-like predator from the deep hijacked our human legacy?

Carlos Castenada describes a "lord and master predator" that imprisons us for sustenance, much as we rear and genetically enhance cattle to render them docile and helpless."

"They give us their mind, which becomes our mind!"[24]

Jacqueline calls these colonists Negative High-Frequency (NHF) Beings – bodiless visitors that arrived on Earth long ago and infiltrated the human spectrum using identity creation technology.

They hacked our minds with thought, hijacking our pure love frequency and flooding us with fears to fracture our psyches.

It's how they developed different identities within a "slave-self setting."

"It wasn't so uncomfortable at first," explains Jacqueline. These suggestions from "nobody" could be "quite accurate." (But) as other influences magnetized into our bio-fields, "it became harder to tell what was you, or something else."[25]

The strength of these NHF colonists lies in their use of highly sophisticated technology. Being unable to thrive for long above ground is their weakness.

What if – having merged their DNA with certain elites for centuries – they had produced hybrid blends in all races through science, medicine, genetics, and technology?

---

24   Casteneda, 1999
25   Oraclegirl.org, 2020

Hybrid humanoids that physically looked just like us, making it hard to differentiate them? That way, they could gain ever-increasing control over us.

What next on the predatorial agenda? Assimilation of life on Earth via mass infiltration? A trans-human type snatch at immortality via injected nanotech?

Could they merge organic beings into an ancient non-human hive-mind affair? Who knew, but they could shove it. I would abstain from the enslavement dreams demanded of me.

If their mind merged with mine, I'd been complicit in the prison construction. I had inadvertently jailed myself. That made me warden and gatekeeper too.

I held the key to my shackles. Escape lay beyond the portals of integrity. Some of my slavish identities continued to argue, but I was still free. Was I about to relinquish my autonomy?

Oh, hell to the no, Siri! Wait. What? You *missed* what I said? Are you *spying* on me?

From here, I'd rely on my wits and withdraw my attention from dissonance. My inner voice would be my source of guidance and authenticity. But which one?

Power lay in perceptive silence. Answers came in the quiet. My physical senses locked me into an intense coffee and high-fat routine, but what was life without your chosen fare to "blunt the edges of despair," as my late Dad would say, after his umpteenth glass of the fermented grape.

Like many close friends, I saw travel as an escape from mundane daily life. Something different, newsworthy, Instagrammable, over *there,* as opposed to here.

International travel became a dystopian nightmare of testing, QR coding, tracking, tracing, quarantining, and goalpost moving. Irrespective of our vax status, European countries closed their borders to South Africans in December 2021.

The loss of my sovereignty was too high a price for travel privileges. I'd stay home instead – better a small queendom than none. I needed a personal reset as the heat of intuitive realizations shattered myriad illusions.

After all, a sovereign queen answers to no one. The lockdown provided the perfect excuse to retreat from society, but I began to feel lonely.

Others had to be going through similar stuff to me. Collaboration bridging differences with unity felt like the key to starting the Facebook Coterie.

Oh, the relief to discover a cyber tribe of sisters, a growing band (width) of far-flung amigas – more than I could have dreamed of – breaking paradigms and following their hearts.

I was not alone in this strange *Brave New World* after all!

Author-artist Donna White described feeling like "being on a fast clipper at sea dodging multiple collisions with refugee-filled rubber dinghies slow-bobbing in the opposite direction."

Others experienced being gaslit by organic portals of the narcissistic variety.

We shared lurching moments of terror as familiar worlds drifted away like helium balloons.

Many of us kept seeing coded numbers 11:11 or 13:13, 12:21 – or adverts on our phones for stuff *we'd only thought about* without an internet search. Nothing made sense, but it mattered not.

Pulsing synchronicity and an inner glow of certainty beckoned sovereign queens who shared Nature's calling to begin our journey anew.

Like Phoenixes, we would arise from the ashes of a fiery rebirth.

FIRE

FORGE *a new way of being with the fire of your inner suns. From here, you're free to be you.*

INCINERATE *fear and pain. Learn to morph in response to the fiery heat of your inner flame. Burn redundant codes of ancestral injuries, beliefs, images, attachments, and subservient identities that shaped your reality with sticks of betrayal. Consign to the flames letter or momentoes that make you sad. Douse any smoldering embers of regret. Farewell can be the purest form of self-love. Scorched earth precedes growth.*

RAGE *and burn off ancestral precedents. Repattern your entire lineage by pinpointing and transmuting family fears and trauma.*

EMBRACE *anguish as an agent of transformation. Explore new paths that lead to an expansion of your reality.*

The Fire Queen

Firing up her courage, she blazes new trails. Her will is her wand.

Quiver of Arrows:
Boldness, courage, confidence, creativity, cunning, determination, destruction, independence, introversion, self-respect, passion, renewal, action.

Archetype:
Freyja, the Aesir goddess of fertility, beauty, war, and death, had a magical gold necklace, a cloak of falcon feathers for avian shape-shifting, and two cats to pull her chariot. Alluring, powerful, and passionate, Freyja could change the course of fate by 'weaving' events into being, a process called Seidr (pronounced "SAY-der). We have her to thank for Friday (Freyja's Day).

REFERENCES:

Whose Magical Tour Is It Anyway?
@newsraters(2020, December 6): bit.ly/339TX6z
Carroll, L (2021) Alice in Wonderland: The Original 1865 Edition With Complete Illustrations By Sir John Tenniel (A Classic Novel of Lewis Carroll) Independently publishedNewGrenada (2021, May 9) Dude in a body bag smoking a cigarette: Twitter bit.ly/3BcPiNP

Chapter 1
Ursula K Le Guin quote, Goodreads
Maitre, DD (2017) The Knysna FIres of 2017: CSIR
Northrup, DC (2021) The Wisdom of Menopause: Creating physical and emotional health and healing during the change New York: Bantum

Chapter 2
Nietzche quote: Lib Quotes
Cara, E(2021, May 26) Testing Lab Asks FDA to Recall 78 Sunscreens Over Carcinogen Contamination Retrieved from Gizmodo: gizmodo.com/testing-lab-asks-FDA-to-recall-78-sunscreens-over-carci-1846977439
Crawford, C (2018) Mommie Dearest Open Road Media
Douglas, GM (2021) Access Consciousness Retrieved from Garymdouglas: garymdouglas.com/
Sunshine on Balls Retrieved from Legendary Strength: legendarystrength.com
History Scotland (2019, March 18) Dragsholm Castle in Denmark: prison of the 4th Earl of Bothwell, third husband of Mary Queen of Scots Retrieved from HistoryScotland: historyscotland.com
Oraclegirl.org, (2021, December 9) Track of the Month 4 Oracle Girl Website: oraclegirl.org
Oraclegirl.org (2021, July 19)
Self Healing Abilities with Dr. Northrup Oracle Girl: oraclegirl.org/library/your-self-healing-ability
Oraclegirl.org, (2022, January)
Kahn, TL (2005) The Reptoid Hypothesis: Utopian and Dystopian Representational Motifs in David Icke's Alien Conspiracy Theory Los Angeles: Antioch University
Keto Cooking (2021, March 17) High fructose corn syrup may block vitamin d, increasing the covid-19 risk of infection. Retrieved from KetoKooking: ketokooking.com
Kruse, DJ (2020, July 6) How Sunglasses harm us - hypoxia and photoreceptor damage Facebook: https://www.facebook.com/drjackkruse
Lawson, CA (2004) Understanding the Borderline Mother: Helping Her Children Transcend the Intense, Unpredictable, & Volatile Relationship, Rowan & Littlefield
Northrup, DC (2021, July 19) Your Self Healing Ability Retrieved from Oracle Girl: oraclegirl.org/library/your-self-healing-ability
PennState (2002, December 11) Ultrasound potentially safe, effective way to kill bacteria retrieved from PennState: psu.edu/news/story/ultrasound-potentially-safe-effective-way-kill-bacteria/
Portnoy, PD (2018, September 12) A flavin-based extracellular electron transfer mechanism in diverse Gram-positive bacteria retrieved from Nature: nature.com/articles/s41586-018-0498-z
Shannon(2019, April 15) 7 Harmful Chemicals Found in Sunscreen shannonsgrotto: shannonsgrotto.com
Spaceagebachelor (2007, January 5)
The Son of God is the Sun of God bibliotecapleyades: bibliotecapleyades.net/mistic/songod_sungod.htm
Standford Solar Center(n.d.) The Singing Sun Solar Center Standford Edu: solar-center.stanford.edu/singing/

Chapter 3

Swiss Policy Research (2022, February 12) The Propaganda Pandemic Swiss Policy Research: swprs. org/the-propaganda-pandemic/

@canadianaco, JD (2022, February 15) Twitter: twitter.com/canadianaco/ status/1493354101232455680?s=20&t=X1m46x2okr-CrcHH8C_Nrg

@KyleTrouble (2022, February 24) Twitter: twitter.com/KyleTrouble/ status/1496833036771823617?s=20&t=lU4u1ii7rwzxBc8bWkXgiQ

@libsoftiktok (2022, February 16) Twitter: twitter.com/libsoftiktok status/1493836876347686915?s=20&t=jTHx8NYaOeVufeYl4OFW6w

Cailler, A (2021, November 10) Brothel offers free '30-minute experience' with prostitute in exchange for Covid jab
Retrieved from Daily Star: www.dailystar.co.uk/news/weird-news/ brothel-offers-free-30-minute-25423249

Casteneda, C (1999) The Active Side Of Infinity Harper Perennial

Chow, D (2020, June 10) Why 'I can't breathe' is resonating with environmental jus-tice activists. Retrieved from NBC News: www.nbcnews.com/science/environment/ why-i-can-t-breathe-resonating-environmental-justice-activists-n1228561

David, DE (2022, January 16) Twitter: twitter.com/DrEliDavid/status/1482776240666951691

Edwards, S (2021, January 22) The environmental impact of disposable masks
Retrieved from Organic Lifestyle Magazine: www.organiclifestylemagazine.com/ the-environmental-impact-of-disposable-masks

Euro Journal (2021) BBC reporter Phil McCann goes viral while covering fuel shortages at petrol station Euro Journal

Fuller, A (2021) Farewell Bill William Shakespeare dies: The first man in the world to receive Covid vaccine dies aged 81 The Sun

godgevlamste (2020, October 10) Crater Earth and The Galactic Scam Retrieved from YouTube: www.youtube.com/watch?v=uz61TubJKJU

Oraclegirl.org. (2020, December 18) Negative high-frequency beings Oracle Girl: oraclegirl.org/ library/negative-high-frequency-beings

IMDb (n.d.) Novak Djokovic Retrieved from IMDb: www.imdb.com/name/nm2980365/ L.P., B (2022, January 16)

Austria to fine unvaccinated in March Luxembourg Times

Margolis, M (2021, September 8) The CDC Just Made an Orwellian Change to the Definition of 'Vaccine' and 'Vaccination' Retrieved from PJ Media

Mathis, MW (2015, December 15) Elvis Aron Presley: From mileswmathis.com/updates.html: mileswmathis.com/elvis.pdf

Mercola, DJ (2021, January 18) Violating Science, WHO Changes Meaning of Herd Immunity
Retrieved from The Defender Children's Health Defense: childrenshealthdefense.org/defender/ violating-science-who-changes-meaning-herd-immunity/

Nal, R (2021, May 29) Nobel Laureate Luc Montagnier - Warns Covid Vaccine May Lead to 'Neurodegenerative Illness' (Video) From Rairfoundation.com: rairfoundation.com/ nobel-laureate-Luc-Montagnier—warns-covid-vaccine-may-lead-to-neurodegenerative-illness-video/

Newstead, A (2021, November 8) You could feel bones breaking": survivors describe Travis Scott's Astroworld tragedy. Retrieved from ABC: www.abc.net.au/triplej/programs/hack/ survivors-describe-Travis-Scott-astroworld-festival-tragedy/13621984

Ramkat, L (2022, March) 2014 to 2022 Retrieved from Facebook: www.facebook.com/LeeRamkat/ videos/334508231950685

RiseMelbourne(2022, January 12) Twitter: twitter.com/risemelbourne/status/1481050107332202496

Sones, M (2021, November 18) 5-fold increase in sudden cardiac and unexplained deaths among FIFA athletes in 2021
Retrieved from America's frontline doctors: americasfrontlinedoctors.org/2/
frontlinenews/500-increase-in-sudden-cardiac-and-unexplained-deaths-among-Fifa-athletes-in-2021/
True, J (2022, January 17) Twitter: twitter.com/jarue369/status/1483187846655664131
VigilantFox(2021, December 18) Twitter: twitter.com/VigilantFox/status/1475632293897285635
Wikipedia (n.d.) I can't breathe Retrieved from Wikipedia: en.wikipedia.org/wiki/I_can't_breathe

SECTION II

WATER

Earth's most potent solvent defies gravity, rises through tree trunks, enables germinating seeds to break through asphalt, expands when frozen, and contracts when heated. Its true power is incomprehensible.

Water is the mirrored blueprint of our reality. By reflecting all colors in its transparency, it shows us what we cannot see.

An alchemical marriage between Fire and Water links your inner suns' golden cosmic intelligence with the waters of your being.

CHAPTER 4

WATER
FLOW

"The relationship between the sun and water is the relationship with the infinity spark."
– ORACLE GIRL

Water can dismantle the scaffolding of your life in an instant – a freak wave washes your child's father off a harbor wall; a heart attack smites your husband, a troll supplants your partner, yanks the rug of affection from your feet with cold, curt announcements.

"I don't love you anymore – not in the way you love me," – a common theme on the Hygge Queen Coterie.

Life's flotsam and jetsam bob up when you least expect it. The best you can hope for when the big wave comes is to "surf over it, instead of drowning in its monstrosity."[1]

---

1   Fitzgerald, 1925

You don't need a surfboard to ride the massive wave that floods into the widening cracks of your eggshell world. You can bodysurf into a pool of self-reflection and wallow for a while. Release the grief that's been tapping your left shoulder for some time.

Your body knows things before your mind computes them. If you ignore the signs, that's on you. Let go already. And flow. What whirlpools of change may await? The urge to continue kicks in. You reach out in the dark. You grab one rung, then another.

You blend with nature's frequency that zaps, assimilates, and reforms unresolved issues. You shed painful precious memories as you climb.

WAVES OF CHANGE

Sarah remembers the day her marriage died. "Talking to him while toweling off after a shower, I caught his undisguised expression of disgust as he looked at me. I had put on weight, as you do.

"Hurt to the core, I sunk into a deep depression for months.

"My recovery started the day our marriage ended. It took months of soul searching. I learned making yourself less will never make anyone love you more.

"As much as he had betrayed me, those parts of my personality that allowed the treachery were as guilty.

"That's what happens when you identify with your neediness and forget who you are. No other person can provide the love my Mother Earth connection ignites in me.

"I promised myself nobody would ever disparage or betray me (or Her) again. My stretch marks are scars of honor from having birthed four children. Now, I see the goddess Gaia when I look in the mirror. And She sees me."

When you choose sovereignty – subject to nobody – your powerful frequency assimilates another slave-self identity.

Going with the flow without fighting the status quo is how you restore yourself. Allowing Water to dissolve all unresolved issues will set you free.

After her husband died of a heart attack in the car on a road trip, Lois Kuhle learned to relish her solitude rather than see it as loneliness.

"Just being near a body of water helped me move from heartbreak into healing," she says.

Adjusting to the "lonely me" after decades of being the "happy we" isn't easy. Rituals, symbolic acts, and words matter, but grief isn't linear. Neither is healing.

Often, it is two steps forward and one step back," says Catherine Lancaster of Dorset, England, who lost her husband Neil to colon cancer after 35 years of marriage.

"Through the mourning, I remembered him with great love. Gradually, I emerged from the depths. Not just as a 'me-on-my-own with a missing half' but as an I Am with novel ideas, tastes, and concepts.

"I love the emerging new Me – she's a merge of the wild, high-spirited young girl I was with the wise woman I'm becoming.

"She is fun, intuitive, daring, beautiful, creative, and a little crazy."

Scottish artist Caroline Morris says she learned to be more comfortable with the uncomfortable.

"When we flow with an acoustic wave, whatever no longer resonates must go, even those we have danced with and loved. No matter whose choice we think it is, it's neither easy nor pleasant being affected by others. I get it, but what if you're not, though?

"Sometimes it helps to look at what you've historically tolerated – all those old patterns, lineages, roles, conventions, and identities you chose.

"Haven't they lived through you long enough? Why not imagine something more expansive that works for both parties?

"Is it crazy to think we're magnificent beings embodied? That we become more awesome every moment?

"That nothing is more potent than we are when we resonate with our true selves?"

TIDES OF ILLUSION

Allowing herself to "flow with the tides of the sea" was how Michaela Mueller of Cape Town enriched her "growth and spirituality" when plans didn't work out as she hoped.

"I had planned to do life the right way. Get engaged, married, have 2.2 children, live happily ever after.

"My wealthy father chalked up three wives and eight children. Drama dogged my childhood for years, something I was determined not to repeat.

"I found the perfect husband – handsome, ambitious, and charismatic. He had an extraordinary love for all women.

"That became a problem, especially after our son was born. Sharing my man was not part of my dreamy plan, so we parted.

"He settled in with his affair, and I went on to meet Gary, a free-spirited, artistic, but naïve Jewish man with limited ambition and a long-standing love for music.

"When our tumultuous two-year affair resulted in the conception of my daughter, I was ecstatic. Gary, not so much.

"He made a feeble effort to mask his shock, but it was clear he wanted to head for the hills. He wasn't ready for fatherhood.

"I said I'd manage alone, and off he went. Six months into my pregnancy, Gary came back. He'd had a change of heart. So had I.

"By then, I'd met a man who provided stability and was helping me grow my business.

"Again, I told Gary I'd manage without him. I could not envisage raising Kayley with next-to-no financial support from someone who would have a say over our lives.

"I look back on it as one of my life's most liberating milestones when being pregnant and unmarried was not the done thing in society. I continued building my business and raising my son in my new relationship.

"I was eight days away from giving birth when my new partner introduced me to his parents at a fancy dress party on New Year's Eve. They froze in horror at my enormous baby bump, shocked beyond speech. I like to think I weathered it all with aplomb!

"When my beautiful daughter Kayley was born, Gary reappeared, asking for blood tests to prove his paternity.

"His request offended me. He hadn't wanted to be a father from the start. Now he expected me to poke needles into my infant.

"Gary finally dropped his request and disappeared from our world again.

"My new partner and I married when Kaye turned two. We went on to raise a family, many challenges notwithstanding. He had a son but objected to my two children having different fathers.

"Eventually, we had a son together. Kaye was six by then and resembled Gary to an uncanny degree. Out shopping one day, we bumped into a friend of his, who gawped when she saw Kaye."

Soon after that, around the time Michaela heard her first husband's fiancée – "the woman he chose while we were married" – was killed driving home from her hen party; she learned a freak wave had washed Gary off the Kalk Bay harbor wall and drowned him.

"I gathered my courage and attended the funeral. When I saw how many people mourned Gary, I felt urged to strengthen rather than untie the connections I thought I'd come to undo.

"Gary's presence felt like a quiet place in my soul. It was a difficult moment, but when his grief-stricken mother welcomed me with love, I whispered I had something precious of hers."

Life resumed, but weeks later, tragedy struck. A man attacked Kayley at a shopping center. Her nanny had taken her to use a restaurant cloakroom while Michaela helped out at another business on site.

Kayley went in alone while the nanny chatted to the restaurant staff at the back. Unseen, the man crept in after her.

Someone eventually heard the little girl's screams over the restaurant music, but Kayley had been badly beaten and abused by the time somebody could get to her.

"It felt inconceivable that such a devastating thing could have happened to my innocent six-year-old girl. A long road of counseling and an eventual bipolar diagnosis lay ahead.

"Kayley never spoke about The Cloakroom Incident through subsequent years of therapy, although she told me she often felt as though somebody was watching her.

"I decided to consult a reputable spiritual counselor with clairvoyant powers who told me Gary watched Kayley 'through his blue eyes' and wanted her to have some of his things.

"She described a pendant with a diver charm he'd been wearing when he drowned and a small inlaid box at his parents' home. She added that Gary's father was not long for this world.

"I called Gary's sister to tell her what the clairvoyant counselor had said. She called me back. Gary's father was ill, but her parents awaited me with open arms.

"It took courage to ask for Gary's things to give his daughter, especially as they had never met her. My eyes welled when his mother took an inlaid box from the mantlepiece and handed it to me. Bringing Kayley to meet her paternal grandparents is one of my most precious memories.

"As we left, Gary's father handed Kayley a gold chain with the diver charm the counselor had described. Soon afterward, he died.

"Kayley and I still share a strong bond with his family."

Sometimes a bad situation can bring something good into our lives. Jacqueline Smidt explains: "A young lady living two properties away from my son phoned an ambulance when she heard gunshots on February 20, 2020.

"This quick thinking saved his life. He had been shot five times in a robbery. When he got out of the hospital, the young lady checked on him at home. They fell in love at first sight.

"Both were in long-term relationships at the time, which crumbled, and in October 2021, my son proposed to her. "Much to my excitement, she accepted.

"So I gained a beautiful daughter, bringing much-needed happiness and positivity into our lives after two awful years. Love will conquer all in the end."

STILL WATERS

Our bodies, the vessels or carriers of our individuation, come and go as designed, but death is not the end. Nothing is lost. Form and materialization renew.

We undo, transmute in nature's cycle of six elements, and generate a new signal, part of a new node on the grid of existence.

"Someone who dies is not lost," says Jacqueline. "The way they are seen and experienced in this universe changes. They turn up at another time-space coordinate within the global nature intelligence system. The five elements the departed drop back into nature for transmutation will reorganize to materialize a whole new version of them."

She compares it to upgrading cars from a Mini to a Jaguar.[2]

In communicating with those who transcend barriers to "tell us they are with us," clairvoyant Reiki practitioner Mel Gouws says death is but an energy shift.

The dead communicate through synchronicities, music, quiet words, and signs you can trust.

Her kickboxing coaches – Mec and his beloved Lyndall, both fit, bare-foot runners – were hiking the formidable Baviaanskloof, an Eastern Cape wilderness area, in December 2020 when Mec suddenly felt too unwell to continue. Lyndall set off to find help but realized she was lost as dusk gave way to darkness.

She had no choice but to remain on the treacherous mountain and wait for the first light.

A feline creature curled up near her during the night – a leopard that moved away when she awoke at sunrise.

Lyndall struggled down the mountain, got help, but returned to find Mec dead.

"Mec began speaking to me from the time I heard the news," says Mel. "He wanted me to tell Lyndall he was still with her.

"I saw his hands touching her toes and other stuff I didn't understand. Coming on the heels of such a tragedy, I had no idea how to approach Lyndall with his messages.

"Both had been atheists and knew nothing of my psychic abilities. I hesitated. Mec shouted in my head. 'Just tell her!'

"I composed a WhatsApp, crossed my fingers, and pressed send.

Lyndall responded, saying she had broken her toes running down the mountain for help. That explained why Mec kept touching them. His messages made sense to her.

"Through me, Mec helped Lyndall cope in her darkest hours. Reuniting their energies was a poignant, humbling experience.

"Fast forward to the present. Lyndall and some of her kickboxing students from the gym were heading back up the Baviaanskloof to build a remembrance cairn for Mec with small stones his friends had painted with messages.

---

2   Oraclegirl.org Track of the month 4, 2021

"I couldn't decide what to paint on my stone and asked Mec.

"E= MC²," he replied.

"Google defined the phrase as being mass converted into pure energy. It was perfect.

"I painted my stone and showed my husband. He laughed. 'Do you see what it spells?'"

A DEEP DIVE

Let me tell you about my mother, Elaine. When she was five and holidaying with her family along South Africa's Garden Route on The Wilderness beach, she ran into the water.

My grandmother bounded into the ocean after her, but a vicious undertow swept them both out to sea.

As the waters pulled her down, my mother thought: "I'm only five, and my life is over. Already!"

Just as her consciousness began to pull away, she felt a pair of arms enfold her. Three youngsters had seen them floundering and pulled them back to the beach for resuscitation.

My grandmother, who lost most of her hearing in the incident, bought each teenager a gold watch inscribed: "Thank you for giving me my life back. With gratitude. Gwen Oosterbroek."

Her last sinking thought she told my mother was that she had married the wrong man. She divorced my grandfather and returned to her true love.

The drowning incident was part of our familial topography, the reason for my grandmother's deafness and my mother's compensatory loud, clear voice that stood her in good stead as a high school teacher.

Fast forward 70 years. My parents retired to Cape Town. They'd been there a few months when pancreatic cancer laid my father low. He was gone within three weeks of the diagnosis, leaving my mother bereft – decades of marriage reduced to a deep, unfathomable silence. As one day blurred into another, my mother strolled up to the communal lounge of her retirement village for a cup of java, where she got chatting with a few of the other residents.

During the conversation, my cousin Ken Oosterbroek's name came up because of a report in the newspaper that day.

An award-winning photographer married to Monica Zwolsman, Ken was filming township unrest in Thokoza when a bullet dispatched by the ironically-named National Peacekeeping Force cut his life short. The 2010 *Bang Bang Club* movie based on Greg Marinovich's book describes those turbulent times.

Ken was my nephew," said Mum.

"Ken Oosterbroek? Are you related to Gwen Oosterbroek?" asked one of the old ladies.

"Gwen was my mother. Why?"

"She gave me a gold watch," came the reply.

They stared at each other across the seven-decade chasm before embracing in tears.

You might consider these tremendous odds, but we are never separate from the elemental power of water consciousness. The waters (and plasma) of our being are in our blood.

SETTING HER ADRIFT

Freelance writer Helen Grange says a stern or disapproving parent plants a compromised seed that becomes a forever-thirsty tree, even when grown next to the water.

"Their attachment patterns become yours. My parents were twice married and unlucky on all four counts. I have no map with a failsafe route to the town of Settled Togetherness.

"I got close to the crossroads of Commitment twice but never got to drink from that holy grail. So here I find myself, a mother, but never once a wife.

"By my 30s, it became clear that my relationship pattern was falling, hard, for unavailable men.

"Their elusiveness ignited the oxytocin storm that would run amok in my veins for months, years even.

"Like an addiction, it would rob me of my life force. By my 40s, my prefrontal cortex had still not subdued my reptile brain to hardwire the value of denying the cake and opting for the salad.

85

"The waters of unavailable men are no place for women with a deep fracture in self-confidence.

"Neither is the end-game a pretty sight. I was a sad-eyed, lovesick shadow of a woman trying to pick up the pieces of what I'd lost.

"I had to do a lot of spring cleaning to feel comfortable again in my body, mind, and soul. My mother's death in 2014 was a gut punch that left me in disbelieving and powerless agony, pushing me unwilling into a dark sea of unknowns.

"My mother was a brilliant, competent businesswoman. While she mentored many over her 76 years, affection was not her main attribute.

"Even so, the empty hollow of her sudden absence gouged so deep it was a physical ache.

"Realizing she was never coming back brought the recognition I had to shift the paralysis and find a fix on a distant shore of healing.

"During grief counseling sessions, I was able to view the highs and lows of our shared history through a zoomed-out lens.

"I had a minor epiphany, detailing the peaks and troughs of our relationship on paper.

"The realness of relationships exists in the twists and turns of daily life, the small compromises in each interaction, as two people assemble their joint barracks against "the slings and arrows of outrageous fortune."[3]

"I found a beautiful photograph of my mother alone in a rowboat on the Ganges river in Varanasi in India, gazing dreamily back at the camera against a soft-focus backdrop of ochre temples and dwellings on the river banks.

"The grief counselor talked me through a closed-eyed visualization of returning her smile, mutual forgiveness, and gently releasing the imaginary rope of her rowboat from my position on the shore.

"I wept many cathartic tears that day, watching her drift away peacefully into a mother-of-pearl horizon in my mind's eye.

"In this letting go, I stopped torturing myself with the guilt-ridden anguish over not being there enough, not doing enough, not saying what I should've said, and saying what I shouldn't have said.

---

3   Shakespeare

"I consciously turned my attention to the highs, the times she stood up for me, her quick humor, caustic wit, and the belly laughs she could invoke in everyone she knew.

"Her enormous generosity at birthdays and Christmases, the stuff of a real relationship hewn in the real world, the ones we honor with profound heartache when it's time to say goodbye."

Time to say goodbye. A world of emotion leaks from the corners of those boxy cardboard words. We pack it all in. Our western culture encourages us to sit on the bulging lid.

UMOYA, THE ZULU WAY

The Zulus of southern Africa have a more interactive relationship with their 'living dead.' Their word for dream or life-force is 'umoya' – easily unbalanced by stress or ancestral neglect.

It's why they revere the "living dead." Their lives are empty without the reverence and ritual accorded to death and their ongoing relationship with their ancestors.

If ignored, the "living dead" will curse the living and endanger their lives.

One of their most pervasive customs involves the buffalo thorn (*Ziziphus mucronata*). Anyone who dies – especially violently – must be helped home by a relative bearing a thorny buffalo branch to snag the person's spirit.

Wildlife tracker Nhlathla Msweli from KwaZulu-Natal explains how it works. "Say, for example, our uncle Siphiwe dies in a car accident. We will bury his body at home, but a relative will go to the crash site with the buffalo branch with thorns that point backward and forwards. It's a reminder for our people to look to the future but not forget the past."

"He will stand at the place of death on the crash site, with head bowed, and speak: 'Mr. Siphiwe, I have come to fetch you. Let's go home together.'

"He will find a taxi and buy an extra seat for the branch, which has Uncle Siphiwe's spirit on the thorn. 'We are taking the taxi now, Mr. Siphiwe. We will cross the river and stop at Empangeni Spar to buy a beer for you and a coke for me,' he will say.

"Back home, the family waits with a goat fed a few leaves from the buffalo branch before being slaughtered. We burn its liver and intestine to ashes for the ancestors.

Afterward, we take what's left of the buffalo thorn to put on uncle Siphiwe's grave. Then we eat the goat."

A robust African concept celebrates the interaction and relationship between the living and the 'living dead' (ancestors) – the continuity of life. "Alive or dead, an African belongs to the clan. Hence the African maxim, 'I belong, so I am.'"[4]

Four Water Affirmations:

1. *Creativity is my current*
2. *The love I give to others overflows from my love to myself.*
3. *Money flows to me like water.*
4. *Waves of wealth wash over me.*

---

4   Ngobese, The Living Dead, n.d.

CHAPTER 5

WATER WORKS

"Our molecular count is nearly 100 percent water,
making us hydrosapiens.
We are Water. And Water is us. We cannot separate ourselves.
What if Water is expressing its consciousness through us?"
— VEDA AUSTIN

Norwegian percussionist Terje Isungset's icy acoustic, spine-tingling symphonies incite goosebumps. Combining Inuit, Sami, and Siberian throat singers with instruments he carves from ice, it's as though Mother Nature herself is ripping, scaling, scatting, and side-slipping in the coolest of cool syncopations.

Isungset's trained ear easily differentiates frozen timbre regions.

The dull, uninspiring sounds a polluted frozen Russian lake produces can't compare with the "gold mine" of pressurized Greenland glacier ice. Artificial, machine-made ice is acoustically dead. Only Nature's ice has musical potential.

Horns, trumpets, chimes, and marimbas are just some of his hand-hewn frozen instruments that "create things I never expected – art by accident. Nature decides the sound," he says.[1]

After his annual Ice Musical Festival in Geilo, Norway, all of Isungset's instruments – "more fragile than glass" – ultimately melt and return to Nature.

"It's part of the concept. Nature is our best friend. If you borrow something from a good friend, you should return it in the same condition."[2]

The wonder of water

The late Dr. Masaru Emoto showed in *The Hidden Messages of Water* how the influence of our thoughts changed water crystals.

"To understand water is to understand the cosmos, the marvels of nature, and life itself," he wrote.[3]

Even so, who knew the water had acoustical capabilities too? As New Zealand water researcher Veda Austin discovered, multi-disciplinary water responds to us in ways scientists hitherto thought impossible.

When the artist and mother picked out some fluff from a water-filled petri-dish before freezing it, the last thing she expected to find was an image of her hand depicted in the ice.

"My rational mind said this had to be a fluke, so I snapped a photo, showed it to my son Rama, and asked what he saw. 'A hand,' he said, looking at me strangely."

That hand image inspired eight years of research and 12 000 more photos, says the author of *The Secret Intelligence of Water: Macroscopic Evidence of Water Responding to Huma Consciousness.*[4]

"I repeated the experiment with seawater, and a fish image decorated the ice. A complex braid image showed when I placed the petri dish above a picture of my daughter's plait.

"The braid hydroglyph, repeated from other angles, was different each time but just as intricate.

---

1   Needham, 2021
2   Morris, 2021
3   Emoto, 2005
4   April 2021

"The water designed imagery specific to music, too. I played *Stairway To Heaven*, and a stairway image formed in every petri dish. The ice portrayed a gong and mallet when I sounded one, responding as though informed molecules worked collectively like pixels creating a photograph.

"The petri dish placed on top of a wedding invitation pre-freezing produced a clear image of a ring. I tried a unicorn and the Latin word for a dagger.

"Accurate depictions of each appeared every time. Van Gogh's sunflowers painting inspired colors and shades in the ice."

Ph.D. Professor Gerald Pollack of the University of Washington, Editor-in-Chief of *WATER*, and author of *The Fourth Phase of Water: Beyond Solid, Liquid, and Vapor*[5] , confirming the structured nature of cell water, encouraged Ms. Austin to use an Egyptian tablet print on three Petri dishes.

"Each hydroglyph depicted the tablet at a unique angle in the ice. I greeted the water, which replied 'hi' on the ice.

"When I asked if the water knew me, the ice copied my signature initials, linking them precisely the way I do.

"Our co-creative communicative relationship blows my mind every time. "Water makes a heart shape whenever I project the word love. We associate love with a heart shape, so water uses that to connect with us. Stressful feelings resembled jagged points. The ice portrayed heartache as a heart within the spikes. Our molecular count is nearly 100 percent water, making us hydrosapiens. We are water. And water is us. We cannot separate ourselves.

Water has shown Ms. Austin at least 25 words, unimagined intelligence, and a potent relationship with everything. At the very least, it is alive, conscious, and listening to us.

"We can understand ourselves as an abstract form of divine intelligence taking the shape of a container it occupies, much as water in a cup becomes that shape. What if Water is expressing its consciousness through our human forms?"

Will there come a time when we can ask a river to reveal a killer in a crime?

---

5   Ebner and Sons

LIQUID MYSTERIES

Pat McCabe, a Dine (Navajo) Nation member, is another mother, writer, and artist who enjoys deep, meaningful conversations with water that "unites and ties us together in such a graceful way."

Concerned she would lose her house when water started coming up from the ground at eight gallons a minute, Ms. McCabe initiated a dialogue with the element "like never before."

Eventually, she told the water to take her house. "You can have it," she said, "because there's something you're trying to do, something my community needs for you to arrive like this. So I will be with you. I will protect you and speak on your behalf."

Ms. McCabe allied with the water telling it: 'You can't flow this way because the neighbors complain you're making things too wet for them ... or because my storage shed is there ... or you will go into the street ... or come into my house. I am unsure what you can do. Water, I need your help. I have to go somewhere now, but I am doing something good."

Three weeks later, when Ms. McCabe returned, she found the water had split in two directions and dropped into the earth to solve her house problem.

The water communicated further.

She should find a lake close to where she lived and pray in it.

"I stood in this long lake singing a prayer song with my drum over the water that told me: 'It's good, daughter, for you to pray into the water because (that) intensifies your prayer. Water evaporates and travels through the clouds.

"So your intention and words can go anywhere they want to go. Maybe they send a little snow down over the Andes.'

"I could feel that the Andes would say: 'Oh! My granddaughter is praying, saying good things, and aligning herself with life.'

"And so, the rest of the life – all of the jungle – would share this intention. The (prayer) you emit into the water travels through the consciousness of this life on the earth. (The element) travels over space and through time because it's the original water.

"We have a closed system, so every person you see – all of our ancestors – drank the same water we drink. (That's how) it unites us in such a beautiful and graceful way.

"So yes, it's a call for respect, but also rejoicing. Look where we are. There's so much magic and mystery around us if we have the eyes to see it. For me, the water is extraordinary and sacred."[6]

Flow forms

Elementor Liesl Haasbroek sees the connection between water and its container as a beautiful relationship metaphor.

"Just as dam water turns stagnant in the absence of movement, a lack of physical or emotional intercourse will cause relationship degeneration.

"Movement is both water's gift and medicine. Transport through pipes and tank storage curtails water's self-healing abilities that rely on rhythmical vortices, spirals, and waves, with laminar flow and tides."

Ms. Haasbroek's flow-form sculptures – "a cooperative of human hands and engineering" – enhance water's ability to increase oxygen levels by designing its preferred movement. It's like having a river with all its enlivening properties in your garden.

"Water has memory and stores everything it has ever touched within its vibrational frequency.

"When working with water in bio-remediation, I could clean out chemicals, plastics, and pollution, but only through movement could I remove the memory of the contamination.

"Water loves to be in a relationship: with plants and trees for their cooling gift of shade, with air that moves and breathes into it. Water can shift anxiety and bring you healing and peace by connecting with your heart. We know and feel it because we *are* Nature.

"We are butterfly wings, rhino horns, rainforest, and desert dust. Water's sensitive skin holds all the information from its environment as we flow through the infinite river of life."

---

6   Uplift, 2017

Liesl's surname Haasbroek means 'fast-flowing waters' in Afrikaans. Ms. Haasbroek was born for this mission, and her passion shows.

A frisson of cognition whispers to the synchronicity of names.

David Broward agrees actions, thoughts, and feelings affect the universal solvent's structure on every level.

His book, *How Water can help you change your life and heal your body*, shows how water records, stores, and transmits electromagnetic data and unites us in an "endless sea of information."[7]

The uplifting effect water has on the human psyche is beyond dispute. While traveling the world studying sea turtles, marine biologist Dr. Wallace J Nicols, author of *Blue Mind*, saw how proximity to water improved performance, increased calm, and diminished anxiety.[8]

"People near water seemed to find healing from anxiety, burnout, or even addiction. I witnessed neurochemistry.

"(Water) takes away all the things on land that distract us; the built environment, the signs, the traffic, the architecture – there's nothing wrong with any of that, it's part of our lives, but it does overwhelm us. It taxes us psychologically, and those things have exponentially grown in the past few decades."[9]

Neurons transmit electrical signals through water in a marriage with fire (sun), connecting all ecosystems. Damage to any one of them ripples throughout the world.[10]

The work of Kurt Wüthrich, Masaru Emoto, Rustum Roy, and Konstantin Korotkov featured in Anna Popova's multi-award-winning documentary *Water: The Great Mystery* prove the element carries footprints and interacts with emotions on a molecular level.[11]

In Other Minds: The Octopus, the Sea, and the Deep Origins of Consciousness, Peter Godfrey Smith studied cephalopods to uncover Nature's self-awareness.[12] Cephalopods are intelligent.

---

7   Broward, 2019
8   Nicols, 2015
9   Niiler, 2014
10   Keepers of the Water
11   Top documentary films, 2006
12   Godfrey-Smith, 2016

Prominent neuroscientists identified their vital neural circuits associated with consciousness in *The Cambridge Declaration on Consciousness*, reinforcing the scientific conclusion that cephalopods "exhibit intentional behaviors."[13]

To me, it's an ongoing elemental puzzle that our human minds may never solve.

RELATIONSHIP AQUATICS

Whatever you focus on, you bring into your reality, so when negotiating relationships, the Water Queen moves the way a mountain stream swirls around a rock.

She either redirects the momentum of an attack towards her vision or shares the current to understand another's point of view. Instead of fighting or renouncing her emotions, she names her feelings. Understanding which of her slave-self identities is experiencing the undesired emotion makes it easier to throw it back into the consciousness stream for dissolution.

The way to tune into someone emotionally is to see yourself through their eyes. Emotionally, we often share the same motivation – to be loved and appreciated. Look at what you feel about someone, and imagine how they might think differently from you.

The Queen learns to listen, observe, and even connect in silent empathy when someone starts ranting. Mostly, the ranting boils down to WITFM (What's In It For Me?).

If you figure that out and supply it to them, you're halfway to resolving any emotional issue.

Behind all helpless, angry rage is the pain of feeling adrift from your Source, a profound self-betrayal. All love stems from Her and, by extension, You.

Self-love is the frequency elevator to loftier realm patterning, whatever you choose to flourish. When Nature is no longer your primary Source, you will accept relationships for the wrong reasons. You will let others exploit, abuse, and drain your precious energy.

---

13   Low, 2012

Every loss can feel like death because it entails the demise of an old way of being, but what doesn't grow must go. It's the only way transformation can take place. It's how Nature works. Resistance is futile.

WAVES OF DEVOTION

For decades, Zanna has used the elements as purification and transformation tools. She calls them her "forever friends" because "working with them allows my energies to update and bring me closer to realizing who I am."

"To purge through the elements is to merge with your magnificence. The body is as divine as the spirit, irrespective of your age. Unveiling your true eternal Self is the most fulfilling thing you can do.

"The ocean's eternal rhythmic motion reminds me to connect the inhale and exhale of my breath. Breathing through my nose filters the air and energizes the nerves in my head. I rediscover myself as a divine embodiment within life's perfect flow.

"Our notions matter because they affect the atmosphere. A belief in scarcity, thoughts like 'there's not enough,' or 'I'm separate, powerless, and what I do doesn't matter' manifest as waste, overuse, greed, and carelessness.

"So don't complain about bad weather. When it comes, welcome the rain. Affirm: I live in a universe that wishes me well and will co-create solutions with me."

Trying to swim against the current will only exhaust you. As Bruce Lee suggests, you slip past conflict when you can 'be water.'

Your power goes wherever your attention flows. What if we saw 'brainwashing' as just another form of Air and Water purification to bring to our awareness the clogged dirt of decades of needing a good rinse? Without water, everything would be dust.

Life, as we know it, could not exist. The Water sustains us in our mothers' wombs, nourishing everything from ants to trees to leopards. The elements shape you, but your light comes from the darkness within.

Six Water Treatments:

*Our emotional connection with water is key to changing how
we treat ourselves.*

1. **ACCEPTANCE:** *Water embraces form and phase transitions
    without resistance. It enters without judgment, whether soaking
    parched earth or quenching thirst.*

2. **SOLVENCY:** *Water's ability to dissolve vital nutrients and pesti-
    cides makes it a good metaphor for maintaining financial liquidity.
    Water moves around whatever it can't absorb. Anything you do to
    water with love, care, kindness, or ritual respect will heal an aspect
    of yourself.*

3. **PURIFICATION:** *Consciously cleanse your aura in the shower,
    swirl negative thoughts, or inharmonious situations down the drain
    every time you wash your hands.*

4. **TAKE A WALK IN NATURE:** *Along a beach, near a river or
    creek as often as possible.*

5. **DRINK FROM A COPPER OR SILVER GOBLET:**
    *A copper vessel positively charges the water and is believed to heal
    wounds, slow aging, fight cancer, and combat arthritis, among other
    health benefits.*

6. **GET A WATER FOUNTAIN:** *In feng shui, using a water
    fountain helps move energies and increase prosperity. Place one next
    to your front door (indoors or outside) to keep the chi flowing.*

Quick Fixes

ANXIETY ANTIDOTE:
30-SECOND NERVOUS SYSTEM REBOOT:
Fill a bowl with icy water, bend over, and put your face in it to activate the mammalian diving reflex that slows the heart rate and calms the parasympathetic nervous system. Ensure the sensitive area above the cheekbone and below the eyes feels the chill to get the best results from this dialectical behavioral therapy (DBT) technique.

Try an icy gel mask over the eye area, run your hands and wrists under the cold tap for a minute, or take a cold shower.

Note: DBT creator Dr. Marsha M. Linehan says people with heart problems or eating disorders (particularly anorexia nervosa*) should avoid activating the dive reflex.*

RELAXATION ENHANCER:
Things to add to your bathwater: Epsom salts, a muscle relaxant, and an anti-aging rejuvenating treatment can provide a deep cellular-level cleanse.
A scoop of ascorbic acid (Vitamin C) will remove chlorine.
A cup of 35% hydrogen peroxide can help you detox.

COERCIVE CORRECTION:
Stop anyone threatening or harassing you with a protective freezer spell: Best done during a waning moon; you'll need a photograph or the person's name written down and a ziplock bag or Tupperware.

METHOD:
Place the image or piece of paper with their name into the container.
Visualize the harasser leaving your life.
Add water or vinegar to the container, seal, and freeze until you notice a change.
If your freezer spell unintentionally thaws, flush it down the loo and start again, if necessary.

CHAPTER 6

WATER QUEEN

"I see that if you try to fit someone in a box, she might slip through the seams like water and become her own river."
– LAURA RESAU, THE QUEEN OF WATER

Memories of Indian Ocean islands lap at the shores of my consciousness – soothing treatments amid the kink-a-choo chatter of bulbuls in frangipani glades. Champagne, lobster, rum on the rocks. Tealights twinkle around a jet bath for two. My husband sinks into floating rose petals with a sigh. Slips on scented oil and sets his hair on fire. Good times!

Fish glint silver in sapphire seas around Sainte Anne; lime-green geckos dart into scarlet hibiscus, golden sunset shawls slip off La Digue's ancient granite shoulders.

The swift shutter of Equatorial night falls. Thought waves bob on currents of nostalgia.

Now, dishwasher steam plumps out my wrinkles, and my tears water wastelands of melancholy.

Many relinquished their sovereignty for a plane ticket, but the jabbed now face the same hassles as the unjabbed.

Quarantines cut into your time and budget at the whim of politicos – another booster for a temporary travel reprieve. Hurry! Only while "privileges" last. Where will it end?

Stockholm works better as a city than a syndrome for me. I dab at the eyes of that clingy, petulant slave identity and jump into my Source connection slipstream.

ROMANCING THE CRONE

A queen needs no external validation or authority. She averts her eyes from duplicitous narratives that demonize her, urging a splurge on pricy products.

Quick! A wrinkle in time saves nine. *This* chemical-laden gunk will extend your sell-by date. Stave off the crone phase that lurks like a monitor lizard in the reeds.

The crone embodies maiden and mother, a trinity of wisdom, fecundity, and purity, bringing love, creativity, intuition, grace, and power to Nature's table.

Yet, the word crone alone conjures visions of a warty witch luring children to her sugar-laden abode where a cauldron awaits.

Who started that malarkey? Isn't that precisely what *they* do? You shall know them as liars by their putrid abuse, spitting hubristic hate, and trading in fear.

Nothing that tries to replicate Nature will ever usurp Her. Laugh if you like, dark corporate sorcerers. Your days are few!

The Source that birthed our Earth was here first. She'll be here long after your demise.

UNVEILING THE GODDESS

"In the beginning ... god was a woman. Do you remember?" So begins Merlin Stone's groundbreaking work *When god was a Woman*[1] , with irrefutable evidence of the cruel suppression of feminine reverence.

Nimrod, the Canaanites, and Abrahamic religions hijacked and weaponized our original story to subdue women and humankind.[2]

Eve became evil and everything in between. Eve's predecessor Lilith is associated with the snake. Rabbinical sources say the Garden of Eden serpent was a hermaphroditic composite of Lilith and her male demon counterpart Samael.

Cabalists called this creature "the Beast." Samuel was evil because of his desire "to unite and intimately mingle with an emanation, not of his nature."[3]

Buddhism, too, is rife with misogyny. Consider some of these disciplines traditionally attributed to Buddha himself, who advised a young monk in the tale of Sudinna: "(Rather) put your manhood in the mouth of a venomous snake or a pit of burning charcoal than a woman." Or "of all the scents that can enslave, none is more lethal than that of a woman."[4]

The clay tablets of the Sumerians (c. 3,500 BC) decree that Nammu – their version of Tiamat, the Babylonian Primordial Creatress – made the heavens and earth from her body.[5]

Nammu birthed An, the Sky God, and Ki, the Earth Goddess, also known as Gaia, Pachamama, Ninhursag, and Hathor, the Egyptian cow goddess, depending on the culture. Names change so much in fragments of ancient history that it's easy to get confused.

---

1   1976
2   Stone, 1978
3   Ha-Kohen, n.d.
4   Pattanaik, 2016
5   Oracc Museum, n.d.

Jacqueline says the story of Genesis refers to the genetic manipulation of humankind and the woman who changed the DNA of an existing native species.[6]

Who was she? What happened to her? Where is she now?

I ponder this in Gozo, where thousands of coral and sea urchin fossils embedded in the island's steep limestone and coralline cliffs speak of an almighty cataclysm.

According to legend, a Mesopotamian god called Marduk, also known as Zeus – 50 names at last count – defeated Tiamat in the mother of all battles, splitting her in half 'like a dried fish.'

One part of her became the earth. The other formed the heavens.[7]

In Malta, remnants of the high esteem afforded the Mother Goddess remain in her 2.13m statue in the Tarxien vestibule and another in Gozo's temple of Ggantija, predating the island's occupation by Phoenicians, Greeks, Romans, Knights of Malta, Turks, French, and the British.

From the flat roof of my parents' three-story farmhouse overlooking the deep blue Mediterranean, a younger version of me scans small stone walls demarcating fields of grazing goats. The breeze ruffling my hair is a caress. A howling gale had lifted me the previous day, still holding my brolly, clean off my feet.

I weighed a lot less in 1994. The village baker had just offered my parents a goat, two hens, a fresh round loaf, and a bottle of honey for my hand in marriage. His five sisters, who rose before dawn to knead the dough, could use some help.

"I see your daughter is strong," said he.

Strong. Like a carthorse? Would he like to inspect my teeth?

"Be my guest if you think you can handle her," laughed my father, "Thanks for the gifts, but we've no room for the livestock."

"We'll take the bread and honey, though," interjected my mother. Seriously?

"Go on, be a sport, Carolee. Their bread's delicious."

It was good. The answer was still no.

It's no coincidence that no and know with a K sound so similar.

---

6   Girl, 2021
7   Spar, 2009

Both either limit or expand your perspective. Belief is the enemy of knowledge, so beliefs have to go. I've seen the lie between the E and the F.

I should have said 'no' more often to weaponized culture – cult rule, fake forests, flimsy vows, plastic palms hiding 5G towers.

No more dancing in paved Paradise parking lots to their tunes and ridiculous demands.

No to exploitation, abuse, and dissipation of my powerful magnetic earth force by heartless beings who abhor Mother Nature.

She will deal harshly with parasitic loosh harvesters who infiltrated our social milieu with images meant to control and constrict women.

Instead of honoring humanity's quintessential force, they gave form to porn to further sever us from our Source.

SEX AND SLEEPING BEAUTY

Sex slops out of every pail in a way that limits, demeans, and pushes women into darker realms of despair.

The entertainment industry serves dollops of FOMO (fear of missing out) with warped, fast-food obsessions, encouraging us to consume the life force of others to make up the deficit.

Ill-treatment of women is nothing new, as anyone who explores the origin of fairytales can attest. *Sleeping Beauty* was about a king raping an unconscious girl.

In Giambattista Basile's essay, *The Sun, the Moon, and Talia*, a king separated from his hunting group finds a castle with locked doors. He scales the wall and climbs into a room.

Finding an unconscious girl – the daughter of a lord called Talia – he rapes and impregnates her. Fairies deliver twins and raise them until Talia awakens.

The king returns to stay awhile with Talia and the children.

When his enraged queen finds out, she orders her guards to kidnap the children – to cook and serve as a meal to their father king. She also tricks Talia into coming to the palace for burning.

The cook spares the children, and the king rescues *Sleeping Beauty* at the 11th hour.[8]

The Disney Corporation sugar-coats and sells the damsel in distress syndrome, a woman unable to survive without rescue, even if the rescuer happens to be her rapist.

It goes deeper. In the poem *Le Serpent Rouge*, translated by Amy Keller, the narrator writes how "In (his) arduous pilgrimage, (he) cleared with his sword (a path) through the inextricable vegetation of the woods (to reach) the mysterious house of the *Sleeping Beauty* – Queen of a fallen kingdom."

The late Tracy Twyman said the *Sleeping Beauty* – a sex magic metaphor – was the embodied (fallen queen) archetype of Venus, entombed in the Pyrenees. The labyrinth – a vaginal symbol etymologically derived from labia – and dense woods proliferate in other Tomb of Venus tales.[9]

In England, 'fish traps' were a euphemism for labyrinths and the Melusine, another half-fish, half-woman figure, lived in a maze. Starbucks anyone?

I see *Sleeping Beauty* as the sacred essence of my internal Holy Grail. That unconscious part of me was kissed awake by a more masculine component needing to act.

Grail comes from the word crater, or creator phonetically. A queen flowing with Source has no use for sorcerers.

Despite how far we've come with #metoo movements and the public unveiling of assorted cads, updated versions of Adèle Syndrome still abound regarding slavish identities.

---

8   Basile, n.d.

9   Twyman, 2004

THE STORY OF ADÈLE

Artistic, gorgeous, and musically adept, Adèle, daughter of writer Victor Hugo, could have had any man she wanted. Instead, she chose a womanizing army officer called Bertie Pinson.

Having had his way with her, he lost interest as commitmentphobes do. The more his ardor cooled, the more her passion for him burned like a wildfire.

"I'll be able to win him over through gentleness," she wrote in her diary.

Stung by his cruel rejection, Adèle followed Pinson to the home of his mistress, where being witness to their urgent coupling pierced her heart 'like an arrow.'

A good girlfriend might have advised her to get off the branch and bark up another tree.

All yearning denotes lack and demands choices, but the fever-stricken Adèle clung vine-like to her illusory oak.

When his regiment moved to Halifax, she disguised herself as a man to stalk him there.

She could have spelled it Hell-ifax for all the comfort it brought her. She pursued him to Barbados, where grief drove her mad.

A former servant found her wandering the streets and helped her return to France, where her father committed her to a mental asylum for 40 years. She died in Paris, aged 85.[10]

Adèle's disconnection with Source forged her belief that only Bertie, the man who broke her heart, could heal it.

When you feel surplus to any relationship requirements, a hybrid identity of the slave-self variety steps up the yearning. You will lie to yourself or try harder to change things, but you may as well leave a hungry Pitbull to guard your steak dinner.

The world of duality provides two sources. One nourishes you; the other feeds off your suffering. Allowing anyone to exploit and abuse you is the ultimate self-betrayal, but it's your choice.

---

10   Dow, 1993

Blood lineage does not bestow loyalty. Habitual patterns of disconnection continue down a long ancestral line.

In this crowded dancehall world of agendas, how many are yours?

Consciously aligning with Nature's principles rather than a synthetic blueprint of what good citizens, aka enslaved people, should do, believe, or follow, is how you maintain mastery over your circumstances.

Master is an anagram for stream, a reminder to flow into your river role and allow powerful love currents to shape and nourish new landscapes. Does the river fear the rocks it flows over and around? Of course not. The sun's radiance outshines every moon and star. No monster can withstand the beam of your inner light.

The star in self-mastery will guide you down that narrow path unencumbered by contradiction and the heaviness of choice.

Whether you're flowing like water, air, or steam, the more you wallow in Mother Nature's vast lake of abundant resources, the greater your replenishment, renewal, sense of joy, and wonder at life. Nothing and nobody will be able to tether you.

This feeling of freedom comes at a price – the deletion of people and things once thought crucial to your wellbeing.

The Queen must face the next part of her journey alone. For many, this feels too painful to contemplate.

Yet, the truth is we are never alone. We are part of a greater whole, never separate from Nature's death, transmutation, and regeneration cycle, so individual mastery and your heart's intentions affect the collective reality. Gratitude opens the gate.

THE TALE OF ELLI

The tale of Elli is a salutary lesson of acceptance. Elli was an ancient servant crone who lived in Jotunheim, waiting on the giant Utgarda-Loki. Depicted with more wrinkles than a Shar-Pei, she embodied wisdom and inner strength.

One day, Utgarda-Loki summoned Elli to the great hall. Here, a sullen Thor, the hammer-wielding thunder god had humiliated himself in a drinking contest, failed to pick up Utgarda-Loki's cat off the floor, and was now challenging anyone in the castle to wrestle him.

Thor laughed when Elli walked in, but he would soon feel the sting of humiliation. Thor fought hard as they grappled each other to the ground, but after a struggle, Elli defeated him.

The moral? You won't beat old age. You may as well stop fighting because Nature will win every time. Getting old is easy.

Trying not to look old is exhausting, expensive, and – let's not sugar-coat things – something will always give your age away.

To dye or not to dye, that is the question. In Act 5 of Hamlet, during the Graveyard Scene, the Prince of Denmark shows his friend Horatio a skull saying: *'Now get you to my lady's chamber, and tell her, let her paint an inch thick, to this favour she must come; make her laugh at that.'*

His words echo in my head every time I stand outside the austere, wind-blasted countenance of Kronborg, Hamlet's looming 16th-century castle in Helsingør, 48km north of Copenhagen.

The lugubrious Hamlet had mother issues, but was he wrong? Why bother with all the maquillage when you only end up as a skull in the ground?

But, BUT, I hear you say. I've been put to pasture in dry grass like a heifer predecessor past her milking years. How now, old cow! If I don't look good, I'll never work again.

Well, go ahead, then. Have the botox. I've been down that road. Who hasn't? The current worldwide anti-aging spend – upwards of $62.65 billion and expected to climb to $88.3 billion by 2026 – only proves the efficacy of the programming.[11]

Youth, speed, and instant gratification are everything. You, on the other hand, are nothing to them. You turned heads once, but you're no longer pretty, nor will you be again.

You have wrinkles, a jelly belly, and a few chins. You splurged on the fillers, and yes, my dear, *of course*, you look younger than, say, Sarah, wife of Abraham, but not *young*, per se.

No matter your hair color, you'll always be grey. Beige, at best. Still a cash cow, though, so fill those lines, plump the lips, a bit of "botox," and "you're good to go." No, they don't say where.

---

11   Statistica, 2022

Emotionally you're parched. Your beloved daughter got snatched Persephone-like to a faraway Hades, beyond your financial reach. Your boss retrenched you after 20 years of devoted service without so much as a fare thee well.

Retrenched – trenched in the mud again like a reincarnated soldier. Who comes up with these words?

So you get the anti-aging treatments. You ratchet up the Facebook likes and Insta-hearts. Your poker face masks the bone-dry inner chasm within a social order worshipping only shiny new things.

"You wonder: 'Wow! Who am I now? After shuffling down life's passage handing out parts of yourself for others to use, you do a stock check and wonder what's left," says Monica Zwolsman.

The good news is there's a lot left. Nature replaces every loss with a gift. Spring buds give way to Summer flowers, and Autumn leaves enrich the dark soil with their falling. New life begins again.

The Queen considers invisibility a liberating superpower and neither laments the onset of gravity nor tries to reverse into orbit like an old space shuttle.

Aging and death hold no fear for her. She welcomes the transition of form and an increase in Mother Earth's consciousness as her inner core merges with Nature's tides of purity, dissolving the parameters of time.

Best friend or worst enemy, it's all you. At least you get to choose the mirrors you'd like to reflect you. No matter what gets snatched from you, it pales beside your sovereign source connection. Everything you decide to attract stems from that.

You need nobody's permission to queen up.

WAITING BY THE RIVER

In Nordic mythology, Loki, the gender-fluid god of Fire, was jealous of Freyja, an archetypal völva or practitioner of Seidr (pronounced SAY-der, from an old Nordic word meaning cord or string) that enabled her to 'weave' events into being and change the fates.

Loki publically disparaged Freyja, accusing her of everything from solicitation to incest.

Did Freyja look to her loom for a revenge tapestry? She did not.

A queen never puts people on the defensive by arguing or disagreeing. She needs neither approval nor abnegation.

Emotional literacy flows. As it happened, Loki got chained to a rock in a dark cave. A snake above his head dripped venom, which his faithful wife caught in a bowl.

Every time she missed a drop, Loki's writhing pain caused earthquakes. Nature saw to that.

"If you wait by the river long enough, the bodies of your enemies will float by," wrote Sun Tzu in *The Art of War*.

How true I have found this to be. Many who condemned me and other sovereign beings as "selfish fuckers and potential murderers" are now dead – some less than three months after proudly displaying their compliance to medical tyranny and its incumbent loss of freedom.

Sun Tzu forgot to mention the scant satisfaction in being proved right. Just a deep sense of sadness and gratitude for their sacrifice.

All those around us are precious. Even those we came to dislike.

Are we not conjugate mirrors reflecting countless angles and perspectives? Reality becomes more fluid when you live in a state of acceptance. When you stop caring how others perceive you and let Nature's World Order sweep those cracked eggshell selves into the compost for putrification – one 't' from purification – you're on your way to a total transformation.

Here's the caveat. While Mother Nature delivers deep knowledge and emotional balm whenever you need it, She brings no cashmere blanket for your feelings. She's not interested in your wounding, crap childhood, closet skeletons, abusive history, and assorted tales of woe. Neither are we. It's beyond boring when you've heard umpteen variations on the theme.

Why hang onto the identity still clinging to that painful event when everyone else has moved on? What's it doing for you? Nature's energy is yours, but why focus on irrelevant details?

She will eradicate the familiar whether you're ready or not. You may as well surrender with grace to Her purification space.

"Each version of you – a hybrid image that comes with different emotional experiences – brings itself to your awareness to allow for purification," says Jacqueline.

"If you can flow with your emotions instead of censoring, changing, or self-diagnosing every time you feel sad or sniffly, you can dissolve the lot by letting Nature take care of it."[12]

Now I resonate with the rocky river bed and pebbles tumbled smooth by rushing water dissipating fears, slave identities, patterns of disconnection, and unresolved situations.

I stream like an eel in Her wake. Water's expansive, free-flowing gift revitalizes and nourishes every aspect of my being. Water can store emotional energy and heal.

Veda Austin's heart shapes in ice formed from a projected thought of love show water's interconnectedness and intelligence – Nature's unlimited store of humor and transcendental wisdom encapsulated in a Petri dish.

Is that why we have "well water?

WATER

WASH *all hard knots of anger, stored trauma, underlying issues, and emotional debris down the nearest plughole, and those versions of yourself addicted to lies, infidelity, unfulfilled longing, despair, shame, or pain. Let it all gurgle down the drain.*

ALLOW *the sun aspect of your being to flush out slavish stagnant waters for Nature's dissolution and replenishment. Love's golden light reflects better on a calm inner lake. The only relationship you need is the one with yourself. Go with Nature's flow.*

TRUST *in nature's transmutation process. If you're not sure how to allow it, get out of her way for now. Wave a cheery farewell to all those tut-tutting friends departing in puffs of piety. Let them go. Resistance is futile.*

---

12   oraclegirl.org

ENTER *the silence for added emotional fluency. Eschew anything not of nature's design and embrace anguish as an agent of transformation. Ebb and rise with her tides of unlimited possibilities.*

RAISE *your words rather than your voice. Rain, not thunder, replenishes the earth so flora can grow — today's tears water tomorrow's roots. Let sorrow dissipate in clouds of steam.*

THE WATER QUEEN

She goes with the flow, embracing the transience of form and phase.

Quiver arrows:
Femininity. Beauty. Intuition. Mothering. Empathy.
Compassion. Emotional literacy. Kindness.

Archetype:
The Greek Goddess Demeter held back the growth of crops when Hades snatched her daughter Persephone and took her to the underworld. Demeter is the giver and taker of life, the reason for the seasons.
She expresses her love and beauty through creativity, art, collaboration, and sensuality, just as trees shed their Autumn leaves to bare their winter branches.

REFERENCES .

Chapter 4 Water Flow

(n.d.). Medical News Today.
Fitzgerald, F. S quote (1925). The Great Gatsby.
Charles Scribner's Sons.
Oraclegirl.org (2021). Track of the month 4. www.oraclegirl.org/library/group/special-events
Ngobese, W. (n.d.). The Living Dead. Retrieved from https://uir.unisa.ac.za/bitstream/handle/10500/1263/01dissertation.pdf (page 3)
Shakespeare, W. (n.d.). Hamlet.

Chapter 5 Water Works

https://en.wikipedia.org/wiki/Water_(2006_film) https://www.resonancescience.org/blog/
Hidden Messages in Water by Dr. Masaru Emoto
Veda Austin website: https://www.vedaaustin.com/
https://www.sodis.ch/index_EN.html
A powerful story from Pat McCabe, a Navajo and Lakota activist.
Source: https://m.youtube.com/watch?v=OeeAMNxuqio
washingtonpost.com/national/health-science/blue-mind-explores-the-calming-effect-that-water-has-on-people/2014/07/28.html
Water, Pure and Simple by Paolo Consigli, MD
Water Consciousness by Tara Lohan
Other Minds: The Octopus, the Sea, and the Deep Origins of Consciousness by Peter Godfrey Smith
https://www.keepersofthewaters.org/blog/consciousness-of-water
https://thesuperyachtlife.com/purpose/calming-power-water/
https://www.bibliotecapleyades.net/ciencia3/ciencia_consciousnature35.htm
amazon.com/Blue-Mind-Surprising-Healthier-Connected/
https://www.amazon.com/Water-Help-Change-Your-Life-ebook/how+water+can+heal+emotions
https://norse-mythology.org/tale-utgarda-loki/
Dancing with Water: The new science of Water by MJ Pangman
https://samcrespi.medium.com/the-gift-emotional-aikido-think-water-be-water-133915c982ce https://www.mindfulnessmuse.com/dialectical-behavior-therapy/how-to-calm-down-from-extreme-emotions-in-30-seconds

Chapter 6 Water Queen

Stone, M. (1978). When God Was a Woman. Mariner Books.
Basile, G. (n.d.). Sleeping Beauty. Retrieved from Pitt.Edu: https://sites.pitt.edu/~
Dow, L. S. (1993). Adèle Hugo: La Misérable . Goose Lane Editions.
Girl, O. (2021). When Eve ate the apple. Retrieved from YouTube: https://m.youtube.com/watch?v=zV–wLWfGZ8&list=PLUve20IxBr4aWti5isz4gEGjaDhtzjuW1&index=7&t=103s
Ha-Kohen, R. I. (n.d.). Lilith in Jewish Mysticism. Retrieved from Jewishchristianlit.com/: http://jewishchristianlit.com/Topics/Lilith/jacob_ha_kohen.html
Oracc Museum. (n.d.). Ancient Mesopotamian Gods and Goddesses. Retrieved from Oracc. museum: http://oracc.museum.upenn.edu/amgg/listofdeities/namma/index.html
Pattanaik, D. (2016, January 6). There's a misogynist aspect of Buddhism that nobody talks about. Retrieved from Quartz India: https://qz.com/india/586192/
Spar, I. (2009, April). Mesopotamian Creation Myths. Retrieved from Met Museum: https://www.metmuseum.org/toah/hd/epic/hd_epic.htm#

Statistica. (2022). Size of the anti-aging market worldwide from 2020 to 2026. Retrieved from Statistica: https://www.statista.com/statistics/509679/value-of-the-global-anti-aging-market/

Twyman, T. R. (2004, October). Le Serpent Rouge Interpreted. Retrieved from Bibliotecapleyades. net: https://www.bibliotecapleyades.net/merovingians/merovingios_renneschateau06c.htm

Oraclegirl.org

SECTION III

Symbolically related to breath, free-flowing Air moves sound, communication, thought, intelligence, inspiration, fresh ideas, and frequencies.

Air feeds Fire, holds Water, and enables your thoughts to take vibratory form in your biofield via an alchemical coupling with the plasmic constituents of your blood.

CHAPTER 7

AIR WAVES

"We are the air purifiers, and we will lift the entire collective."
– DR. CHRISTIANE NORTHRUP

Unblocking and redirecting energy through chanting has been around for eons. Om to that! We sing the body electric as we heal through a-tone-ment. In the beginning was the word, which created the universe. Or so they tell us. Let's be clear. It's their story, not ours.

Whoopty do! While it sounds good in theory, how can it be true when there is no beginning and there'll be no end?

Were these whoppers supposed to snatch power from us under the guise of religion? I'd stake my life on it. Perhaps I did – in another time and place when priests burned women just for prescribing nature's remedies.

What if they use sound to keep us in line? How might that happen?

SONIC PRESCRIPTIONS

From Verdi to Mozart, the world's greatest classical composers relied on Solfeggio frequencies.

Tibetan monks used the pure 432Hz tone that resonates with Phi's golden mean to transmit healing energy in their hand-made singing bowls. Unifying the properties of light, time, space, matter, gravity, and magnetism with our DNA codes, biology, and consciousness, magnifies our connection to nature.

So why was this pitch standard changed from 432 Hz to 440 Hz?

The latter does not harmonize on any level corresponding to the cosmic rhythm or natural vibration. Was it a way to weaponize sound against us? Did Nazi propaganda minister Joseph Goebbels want to imprison people within a certain consciousness?

Leonard G. Horowitz writes that Goebbels instituted the 'allegedly superior' A=440Hz tuning as standard three months before Hitler invaded Poland on September 1, 1939.[1]

Color and sound influence our health. Is it unreasonable to assume the music presented to us tunes or programs us to be a certain way? More pliable, say, or susceptible to discontent? Who knows? Napoleon said history was a "set of lies agreed upon."[2]

Self-curating your news, entertainment, and music feeds instead of relying on the mainstream offerings *du jour* is how you start deflecting stuff that's not yours.

Pythagoras introduced the Ancient Egyptian correlation of musical qualities with quantifiable numerical values to the western world. Sacred buildings used the 1.618 golden ratio to connect with spiritual realms through resonance. Energy-emitting pyramids and dome shapes produce a penetrating radio wave (named negative green) that carries vibrational sound information to resonate with "higher realms in prayer."[3]

Acting as antennae, capacitors, and resonators, Gothic Cathedrals harvested free electromagnetic energy from the environment and bathed

---

1   Leonard G. Horowitz, n.d.

2   Bonaparte, n.d.

3   Karim, n.d.

previous civilizations in bell and organ resonance to promote health and harmony. Church bells used coherent sounds to transmute darkness into light and dispel heavy energy before wars, fires, and mud floods erased this old world architecture, culture, and most of its bells from history.[4]

Solfeggio frequencies, dating back to Pythagorean times, were incorporated into hymns and Gregorian chants to induce specific blessings on anyone who listened.

Today, even mainstream medical professionals advocate the Solfeggio scales to promote healing. Research proves that classical music can increase red blood cells in vitro and prolong cellular longevity.[5]

Solfeggio Frequencies & Associated Benefits

40 Hz — *stimulates an increased neural response to fight symptoms of dementia.*

174 Hz — *reduces pain and stress.*

285 Hz — *activates cellular regeneration, healing of cuts and burns*

396 Hz — *transforms fear, guilt, and grief into more joyful emotions*

4096 Hz — *purify your home, office, and energy field*

417 Hz — *removes traumatic energies and dissolves blockages.*

432 Hz — *boosts spiritual development, emotional literacy, and mental clarity.*

440 Hz — *triggers cerebral and cognitive development.*

528 Hz — *known as the miracle tone, promotes blessings and DNA repair.*

639 Hz — *produces positive feelings, transparent communication practices, harmonious interpersonal relationships, and situational awareness.*

741 Hz — *promotes creative expression and solutions to problems.*

852 Hz — *redirects the mind from intrusive, negative thought patterns that cause depression and anxiety. Promotes spiritual enlightenment.*

963 Hz — *activates the pineal gland and energizes a strong Source Connection. It's known as the frequency of the gods.*

---

4   Shore, 2014
5   Hungerford, 2019

Pitch Perfect

The mathematical – some say *mathemagical* – patterns in music can "take people out of themselves," as Elton John put it[1].

The vibrations that sound emits will either benefit or harm the listener.

"Music is a spiritual thing of its own," said Jimi Hendrix back in 1969. "You can hypnotize people with music, and when you get them at the weakest point, you preach into the subconscious what we want to say."[2]

Research shows when we listen to music, we harness the 'healing power of sound to energize, motivate, comfort, or soothe our minds and bodies.'[3]

Like frequencies of light in a color spectrum, sound, too, has a set of sonic hues. You've heard white noise, but who knew there was also pink, blue, violet, red, green, and black noise?

Pink noise promotes sleep induction and also benefits memory improvement.[4]

Blue noise promotes better vision. Violet noise can treat tinnitus, while various applications from acoustics testing to electrical engineering use the other colors.[5]

Like the sun and sky or the Ukrainian flag, blue and yellow are used therapeutically for serenity-inducing and nerve-strengthening properties[6].

Chromotherapy is nothing new. Color tuning is a type of visual cymatics. Is that why mosques use such colorful tiles inside? Some devout Muslims say the Koran was designed to be sung and heard as a healing instrument. Sounds heal people.

Music can spark epiphanies. Matrix Energetics practitioner Wendy Leppard recalls listening to Pink Floyd's *Dark Side of the Moon* on

---

1 John, n.d.
2 Robin Richman, 1969
3 Boothby, 2017
4 MacMillan, 2017
5 Geere, 2011
6 Giorgio, 2014

headphones when the phrase 'there's more than this' popped into her mind, kick-starting her journey into the remedial art of sound.

Your voice, alone, has healing powers. Lullabies – mothers crooning to their children – are older than time.

Sound can raise consciousness levels, which might explain why chanting connects with "ritual, primitive ... first stages of religious expression."[7]

As American developmental biologist and author Dr. Bruce Lipton might agree, I'm in good company now that I identify as a radio station operating from a wider bandwidth than before.

He says our brains act as tuning forks. We interpret vibes through our internal compass and broadcast them out again.

Programmed to listen to other people's words, we distance ourselves from nature's innate wisdom.

"All of our issues are unconscious, invisible, and coming from ourselves. Unless we know that, we're stuck forever. People need to see this invisible influence on their lives."[8]

Lynne McTaggart agrees this is likely how we came to our psychological inheritance.

In her book *The Field*, she presents a picture of an interconnected universe in which "all living things are a coalescence of energy ... connected to every other thing in the world.

"This pulsating energy field is the central engine of our being and consciousness, the alpha and the omega of our existence."[9]

SINGING THE BODY ELECTRIC

"Our true essence is electrical. That's why we say the light has gone out when somebody dies," says Eileen McKusick, an internationally-recognized thought leader in therapeutic sound.

Her books *Tuning the Human Biofield, Electric Body, Electric Health,* and the *Biofield Anatomy Hypothesis* detail her 26-year research into drug-free ways to treat pain and restore systemic balance.[10]

---

7   Melanie Braun
8   Lipton, 2014
9   McTaggart, 2003
10   McKusick, The Books, n.d.

Using sound like sonar, Ms. McKusick found the tones could modulate the biofield's physiology in vibratory patterns related to our emotional and physical states. She says the struggles and stressors of childhood and getting older remain in our energy fields.

We live in an energy-based reality. A specific frequency drives every e-motion – energy in motion – the force behind manifestation. When we identify with our wounds, we create a wounded self-image. However, uncomfortable, guilty, or shameful emotions help us stay balanced.

"Isn't the inability to feel shame and admit wrongdoing the definition of a narcissist? A person who can't feel ashamed of bad behavior is not someone we want to be. When expressed in healthy ways, guilt and shame can help us regulate our behaviors and motivate us toward positive change where appropriate."

According to the *Biofield Anatomy Hypothesis,* a double layer 12-banded membrane confines our torus-shaped biofield extending about 1.5m to either side of the body and three-quarters of a meter above the head.

Twelve strands in each band result in a flow of 144 "cords of light" circulating through our system at all times.[11]

Ms. McKusick says a bi-directional energy flow of negative electricity from the Earth's surface and a positive charge from the atmosphere and sun courses through the central channel and around the field's outer double-layer boundary. Traumatic memories, stored in standing waves within the biofield's boundaries, create pockets of distortion and resistance in the energy flow.

"Recently-generated memories are close to the body and move away over time. We find the information on gestation, birth, and infancy just inside the membrane.

"All other experiences fall in between, like rings in a tree. Different regions store information about emotional experiences. For example, sadness, grief, and depression can weigh us down, creating pain in the left shoulder.

"The energy of our memories contains mass and charge. When we accumulate too much of a particular emotion, our electrical system can go out of balance (and) affect the physical body.

---

11   McKusick, 2019

"Tuning forks are used to scan the biofield to locate areas of distortion and resistance. Their coherent input helps the body resolve the noise and release the associated tension.

"The energy-adding 'charge' to a particular memory can be released from that pattern and guided back to the energy center to enhance the overall flow.

"The restoration of frozen energy back to flow can decrease pain, relieve heavy emotions, and increase the overall voltage of the system, resulting in more resiliency, excellent immunity, and a brighter outlook."

Biofield Tuning or Sound Balancing is the 'syntropic process of bringing lost life force back into our bodies' using tuning forks to track patterns in the biofield magnetically.

Subtle sound changes, distortions, and the current flow tonal quality inform the practitioner of any discordant vibrations.

Happy experiences are also easily reverberated for an emotional reset.

"Think of it as entropy versus syntropy. Entropy is losing order over time, while syntropy is the restoration and creation of order.

"When you're feeling out of sync, the simplest way to get back into alignment is through your body's inherent music or heart song.

"Sound therapy can help you tap into – and transform through joy – the electromagnetic flow of information in and around the body."

In perfect harmony

We each have a unique sound. That's how voice recognition technology works. When the body is out of tune, the mind can become foggy and compromise the immune system.

While orthopedists use tuning forks to detect stress fractures in large bones, Biofield Tuning accelerates transformation by restoring our electromagnetic system and increasing our Source Connection.

Engaging the vibrating symphony of waveforms that make up the body's electrical and acoustic systems awakens our music and restores harmony. It helps us access feelings of clarity and empowerment that guide us back to optimal health.

Our bones are dynamic, crystalline, and piezoelectric. Coaxing our inner music back into coherence helps us access our divine blueprints.

The body's natural energy flow feeds the nervous system and oxygenates the blood. Healthy cell functioning is optimal with a pH-balanced body voltage. Clinicians have found certain types of music, toning, chanting, tuning forks, singing bowls, magnetic waters, frequency generators, and phototherapy treatments can improve tissue water structuring.

Sounds imprint every cell, something bio-acoustic medicine and cymatics prove.

Stanford University researchers have identified acoustics that can manipulate cells into intricate patterns and create new cardiac tissue to replace damaged heart parts.[12]

High precision acoustical generators use sounds to create, harmonize, cleanse and release. We can use our voices and acoustic instruments – natural harmonic sounds – to apply the same principles.

Quartz bowls were initially made as silicon receptacles for the computing industry; they, too, produce a calming tone when struck.

Sonic cuddler Wendy Leppard's singing bowl meditations restore harmony and balance with their calming notes.

"We create whatever we perceive," she says. "We are infinite, expansive, multidimensional beings. When the fear of death no longer grips us, we move beyond ridiculous restrictions."

A regular sound bath does for the soul what a water bath does for the body. Anyone bio-energetically out of whack can tune in to reinstate a sense of wellbeing.

Our disconnect from nature – 'our deviation of forgetfulness' – allowed something else to replace our innate signaling and open the door to dis-ease.

"Centering our frequency into wholeness and coherence is one of the most powerful ways to facilitate positive change," Wendy says.

"There is no difference between religion and spirituality. If you are not working directly with your body, you're wasting your time.

"People not present in their bodies or those who get drawn down paths of distraction – rearview mirror stuff – lack coherence.

"Singing bowls work directly with Mother Earth's frequency to realign your original biofield blueprint.

---

12 Armitage, 2018

"When we surrender to the sound, we expand our awareness into infinity. Chi or life energy can flow freely, clearing, balancing, and restoring the body's rhythm.

"The flow of frequencies produced by tuning forks, gongs, crystal bowls, or even the voice help release hormones and feel-good endorphins that return you to coherence.

"The more you listen to the clear tones of the bowl and sense the spaciousness within you, the more your body surrenders into its natural balanced way of being.

"Words may be ambiguous, but vibes never lie. The love from your frequency is the purest love there is. It comes from you – nobody else can give it to you. It enables you to trust your inner guidance, liberates your natural expression, nourishes, nurtures, and supports you.

"We're here to fully connect with nature's frequency, facilitate a new way of being from our heart space and hold the vision of what we'd love to create for ourselves and the Earth. Our biofields can bring into coherence and transform whatever we engage with.

"The moment we put awareness into our observations, we can shift them.

"We do this by suspending judgment of ourselves, being present, and basking in our radiance within an expanding connection grid.

"This goes way beyond the stories we create about ourselves through childhood conditioning and perceptions limiting our perspectives.

"Removing the distractions, purging everything you're not, will facilitate a more rapid transformation.

"Wisdom comes to you when you go within, listen, and attune to your naturally coherent frequency. The guidance shows up in myriad ways.

"Forget what you think you know. When you choose to connect and engage in the space of what you don't know, magic can unfold.

"There is nothing else out there. We are alchemists who can change anything. We are walking symphonies - harmonious compositions of light, information, and music, expressing our home note and heart song.

"Our radiance spreads joy, gratitude, and love.

"Expressing our uniqueness with delight is how we make a difference to the world."

Cheryl Corson, a Peter Hess Sound Massage practitioner and US National Board Certified Health and Wellness Coach from Lancaster, Pennsylvania, says sound healing leads remedial exploration today.

Practitioners tap singing bowls on a clothed receiver's lower back, foot soles, or elsewhere on the body for about a minute, releasing soothing vibrations.[13]

---

13   Hess, n.d.

Nine resonant code crackers:

1. **USE YOUR INTUITION:** *Information is static without intuition. Sounds become clear when you listen with your inner ear.*

2. **STEP IN ANOTHER DIRECTION:** *Shift your thoughts into a new reality by moving your hands, eyes, and feet. Choose another pattern. Only drama addicts keep gravitating towards their lack of self-worth and victimhood.*

3. **COMMAND YOUR ENERGY:** *Control what you experience by realizing your feelings belong to an identity, not you.*

4. **CHANGE YOUR FOCUS:** *Choose lighter, more playful moments to transform your world.*

5. **ATTRACT WHAT ALIGNS:** *Never embody discordant energies to fit in. Resonate with joy and gratitude.*

6. **AFFIRM CONSCIOUSLY:** *Change your script. Whatever you say about yourself is what you'll be. Act as though what you want to happen has occurred.*

7. **CONTINUE IN THE PRESENT:** *Judging anything by how it was has you searching for pain when anyone mentions a trigger. Not helpful.*

8. **SURRENDER TO COHERENT VIBRATIONS WITHIN YOU:** *Your body knows the truth. You are whole and complete as you are. There is nothing you have to fix. Be your authentic self.*

9. **MOVE PAST DUALITY CONCEPTS:** *Experiences you label positive, negative, happy, or sad make no difference to your frequency, which exists at a perpetual setting in space-time reality. Change radio (or train stations) instead.*

Four Air Affirmations:

1. *I tune into the frequency behind each narrative.*
2. *I attract more of my dream life when I reclaim and speak to power.*
3. *My body is a finely-tuned instrument in a cohesive orchestra.*
4. *I can do anything when I stay true to myself.*

CHAPTER 8

AIR VENTS

"The question is," said Alice, "whether you can make words mean so many different things."
– LEWIS CARROLL
IN THROUGH THE LOOKING GLASS

Words are double-edged swords that can heal, impair, free, or enslave. The blade designed for mass confusion can change your paradigm and life patterns when you see/sea/c the harm in words twisted by magick to charm.

Advertisers and marketers have used "word spells" on us for decades. Weaponized anthropology, if you will, in covert persuasion.

Grammar and the grimoire both use spelling to enchant. Words are the birds and the bars that cage them. Now I see why 'icy' is so easy to spell!

Learn to see through corporate magick techniques and render them redundant. Adapt some of their strategies to bring about desired results or shrivel their trickery in the heat of your glare.

No secret remains hidden forever. You turn their tables when you become aware.

GODDESSES PUSHING PROFITS

Just Do It! Are you thinking about Nike right now? This winged Greek goddess of victory has a United States Army ground-to-air missile named after her.

She's part of the hood ornament on all Rolls-Royce vehicles, Honda Motorcycles use her wings as the inspiration behind their logo, and of course, there's the sports company that uses her name to flog footwear.

Bit of a come-down, if you ask me, especially when Red Bull gives you wings! Just as I wrote the Red Bull remark, my WhatsApp pinged with a joke cartoon from a friend saying: Dead Bull gives you biltong! (Jerky). Does the AI have a sense of humor, too?

Nike's name originates from 'Neikos' and 'Neik,' meaning struggle and attack. The Roman equivalent of Nike is Victoria.

Is Victoria's secret hermaphroditism? Corporate advertising and policies push increasingly gender-fluid narratives. Is it all in the long arms and the jaw?

The Greek goddesses Aphrodite and Hera inspired Unilever's Dove brand and the NBC Peacock logo.

Versace based their logo on Medusa, the snake-haired goddess who could petrify men with a glance. As superpowers go, I like it!

Starbucks adopted the Melusine – the siren mermaid representation of Venus – to sell coffee.

The late writer-researcher Tracy Twyman said 'invented' Greek Mythology explained the Book of Genesis from the outcast Cain's perspective. Her research points to Grail kings of the ancient world participating in vampiric sex rituals with "Venus herself, 'Queen of Harlots' and head of the temple prostitutes."

She believed the Greek and Roman goddesses – "fallen angels" trapped in the underworld – worked with corporate magicians to attempt a universal alchemical reset that would defeat humanity or incorporate it once and for all.[1]

If this is the force behind "communitarianism" or the "great reset" of the globalists, it begins to smack of desperate coercion on their part. For centuries, their goddess archetypes and genius phonetics system have harnessed human energy and directed emotional flow.

The more we awaken to our innate power, the less corporate magicians can entrap and control us.

Word Magic and deaf Phoenicians

Words – their sound, vibration, and frequency – are what whirl reality into existence. The Greek word logos, an "agent of creation," is the "active rational and spiritual principle that permeates all reality, (acting as an) "intermediary between God and the cosmos."[2]

As cymatics proves, you – the dreamer-creator – shape or give form to concepts every time you pronounce certain words – wittingly or unwittingly.

The Egyptian belief in the power of language to affect the world comes across in the Pyramid Text, Coffin Text, and Book of the Dead.[3]

In his Roman treatise De Eloutine, Demetrius describes ancient Egyptian vowel chanting to praise the gods by uttering the seven vowels in due succession. "… men listen to it in place of the flute and lyre."[4]

The Egyptians used the seven vowels from the Oriental languages as musical characters engraved on their walls. Central to the soul of Egyptian magic was the belief that words and vibrations could disintegrate matter.[5]

"The sound of spirit striking the air and declaring a person's whole wish … a sound full of action."[6]

Word contradictions keep us within a prison-like frequency. Contra is 'against or in opposition to.' Diction means speech and trumps definition.

---

1   Twyman, n.d.

2   Britannica, n.d.

3   Britannica, n.d.

4   Oakie42, 2022

5   Braun

6   Source: Brian P. Copenhaver, Hermetica (Cambridge University Press, 1992), pp. 78 58.

It's why we have a dictionary rather than a definitionary. It's a 'pronounced' effect.

Sun and Son are not just phonetic matches. Ra, the sun god's name, arises in words like rays, arms, radio, Abraham, Sarah – in English, Latin, Germanic, and Scandinavian dialects.

Sanskrit, ancient Egyptian, and Arabic all influenced the European languages. The word 'desert' in English, for example, is similar in French, Spanish, and Italian *(desert, desierto, deserto)* and "*dšrt*" (pronounced de-shret) in ancient Egyptian.[7]

Words ARE spells. Magnetic without the 'net' gives you magic, but some words seem designed to trip us at every turn. Good morning! Are you awake?

Or, are you putting the 'fun into the real' (funeral) party for the mourning? Post cremation, your ashes go into an urn. And for this, you earn your keep, so bring on the weekend. Can't we say 'strengthened' or is it the end of the weak?

Hello! O-hell? Might I be progeny – daughter – of Helios, the Greek word for sun, or sol in Latin? Religions claim to save my soul, but I have my solar plexus.

I take in the grounding elixir through the soles of my feet. Why would I require a censer-swinging priest?

We've learned to revere and fear many gods, but Nature needs no religion or ties that bind. El, a shortening of the plural Elohim, is a generic word for god in many languages meaning Supreme Being. Why favor one gender over another?

Why Elohim and not Elo*her*? *The Winner Takes It All* pops into my mind's jukebox. *Money, Money, Money* follows. Then, *I Wonder (Departure)*. Wait. I see 'der one' in wonder, but why Abba?

I Google its meaning. It's Father in Aramaic. On the B-side to *The Winner Takes It All* is my biological mother's name – Elaine – and the El again.

Inserting the phonetic letter L into 'word' trance-forms it into 'world.' The word 'elderly' originates from the old Norse tale about Elli,

---

7   Mina, n.d.

the servant crone whose wisdom and hidden strength enabled her to defeat the mighty Thor in a wrestling match.

The sound of a language is literal magick. Abracadabra! The Aramaic word means: I will create as I speak.[8]

The Phoenicians – master magicians, maritime traders, and inventors of the Royal purple – originated the Western, Egyptian, and Greek alphabets, inventing words with double and triple meanings.

In that way, those with insider knowledge could glean a different intent behind the spoken or broadcast words while maintaining plebians on a single, more controllable level of understanding.

A definition sounds like a deaf Phoenician.

Worship or warship?

Were religions designed to lead us into compliance? Why do the words worship and warship sound so similar? Even The Lord's Prayer, which we learned by rote as children, might have led unsuspecting ears into another agenda.

While my little sister used to mispronounce "lead us not into temptation" as "lead us not into the station," artist-author Donna White finds the ending more disturbing phonetically. "Forever endeavor. A lifetime sentence. No reprieve."

The "deliver us from evil" line puzzled me. Added to any verb and its derivatives, the letters 'de' reverse, sever, or remove the meaning. Demean it. So to de-liver us from evil could be construed to free us from the liver, an organ Ancient Greeks and Romans believed hosted the soul – "the fire that burned perpetually in the human body."[9]

Buddhists correlate 'desire' with suffering. To 'de-sire' something is to neuter or render it impotent.

Some Coterie queens dispatched their problems by discussing them in the past tense. When you change "I fear success" to "I feared success," the ed (or de) removes the fear.

---

8   World Wide Words, n.d.
9   Orlandi, 2018

A corona, which means a crown, is the circle of light around the sun or moon. A halo in art illustrations expresses a person's holy luminosity or divine majesty. We crown kings and queens at their coronation.

My corona is the power of my inner sun. Jacqueline describes this "relationship between your pituitary and pineal glands" as "the light of you," our "plasmic aura, the glow of our material presence," a manifestation of the "pure love" gold frequency.[10]

Helios and Apollo symbolize various aspects of Omicron, the enclosed power of the sun and fountain of all energy on Earth. Omicron's circular form reflects the sun's disc and symbolizes Christ as the bearer of eternal light.

In the 1963 *Omicron* movie, an alien parasite infiltrates a human body to enable the rest of his kind to conquer the human race. And in *Omikron*, the 1999 video game, David Bowie's character warns the people they're becoming government puppets. "Join the awakened ones, and rise to fight for your freedom. Together, we can win."[11]

In late November 2021, Omicron, the coronavirus variant, brought international travel to a standstill, even though it proved to be no more dangerous than a cold.

Omicron also anagrams into moronic and oncomir, a microRNA associated with cancer. An encoded con?

A ruse? How ironic to urge such Draconian sovereign-depriving restrictions in its name. Just a coincidence, I'm sure.

Remove the RNA from the Pfizer RNA vaccine, Comirnaty, and you get Comity, which means 'an association of nations for mutual benefit.'[12]

Delta Omicron also spells out Media Control and Demonical Rot. And is it just a coincidence that 'influencer' sounds like 'influenza' or atmosphere like 'at most fear?'

---

10   Jacqueline, oraclegirl.org2021

11   Bishop, 2021

12   Comity, n.d.

WORDS ARE SPELLS

The scales fell from Dr. Christiane Northrup's eyes when massive 'Vitamin See' doses restored her sight.

"The Divine has a great sense of humor," she says.

The eyes – they see. Be silent to listen. Gin or djinn and tonic? Both are spirits. From depression, I pressed on. Mathematically, 'eleven plus two' equates to 'twelve plus one.'

Anagrams are fun. However, when you pay attention to how corporates use words as weapons, you see through their attempts to break and rebuild you – via broadcasts, ads, and mainstream articles – into a dependent, dependable consumer. Buy into their agendas, wave farewell to your sovereignty. Buy, bye!

Everything – phones, cities, watches, and household appliances – is smart today, but here's the word's etymology.

In Middle English, it was smerten. In Danish, it is *smerte*, with variations in other languages. It means "to feel or cause" pain.[13]

Why would that be, I wonder?

Our entire language is spellbinding. It's all in the phonetics – another homage to the Phoenicians – like the fiery tail feathers of a phoenix rising from the ashes of its funeral pyre to symbolize rebirth and renewal.

Phone IX is also an anagram for Phone 911 – if you read the IX as nine and the XI backward as 11, one of life's little quirks.

Grammar combines words to create sentences with the right – or rite – spelling, while a grimoire mixes magickal symbols to cast spells.

The word hours is an anagram for Horus, the cyclical solar god, hence the word horizon. The intentional misuse of words to alter perceptions and coerce people into acting against their own best interests used to be known as 'lies and deceptions.'

Now it's more indulgently called 'spin' – another loaded word that (to me) conjures an image of a spinster weaving her magic – *Seidr* – from a spindle.

Used dismissively, the word spinster implies a woman not particularly attractive to men. Bless! Hah, I hear 'be less!'

---

13   Wiktionary, n.d.

Words are swords. Sharpen your tools and watch what you speak into your existence. Might (mote) it be that those who control things from the shadows fear feminine power? Just a thought.

CURRENT SEAS

Commercial words come from the ocean, where the choppy waters of maritime law govern every aspect of an endeavor.

Take merchant. Mer means sea in French; chant is a repetitive sound. Thus, the merchant sings a 'song of the sea' hoping for 'repeat' customers.[14]

Repeat is linked etymologically to 'feather' (Latin' *repetere*.) Vati is the Sanscrit word for 'feather,' and German' father' – feather without an 'e.' Vati appears again in Vati-can. The 'holy see/sea' or Papa-sea (papacy) refers to the pope. So far, so paternal, but how does payment come into it?

The transitive verb, 'pay,' comes from the Latin *picare* meaning 'pitch,' a type of tar protecting boat hulls from water leakage.

Tar is another word for sailor, as crossword fans might know. To pitch something means to float an idea, as in a sales/sails pitch.

In old English, float meant boat, but it's also a type of cash register. Nobody wants to drown in debt at the mercy of loan sharks charging an arm and a leg.

A sails man adjusts the sails. A commercial salesman does the same, especially in times of emergency – emerge-in-sea. People are thus encouraged to 'blow their currency' so the business can avoid 'liquidation' or exposure of any lie-abilities.

To 'liquidate' a competitor is to kill or eliminate them with debt. Phonetically all ships are Liquid Dated with a certificate of manifest or origin related to the cargo.

Censorship is a means of suppressing any materials deemed politically incorrect or a threat to the state. Censor sounds like censure (blame or reproach), sensor (detect and alert), or even censer, an incense burner used by priests.

---

14   Last, 2014

Humans are birthed or 'berthed' from maternal hips – a ship anagram – and our birth certificate deems us the property of whichever government captains the Citizen Ship.

Not exactly what I'd call a friendly relationship.

With her penchant for whimsy, Laurel Airica, a Diction Recovery Specialist, writer-poet, and English linguist, eavesdrops on the unheard words that "echo through our double talk and wRITES that set off lasting rePercussions beyond our spoken inTensions."

"Turn LOVE around. We get the primary letters for the word EVOLve. Love is the evolutionary force that brings opposites together to create new life.

"Thus, LOVE and EVOLve, when woven together, intertwine like the strands of DNA to depict the basis for life. DNA, too, has meaning in reverse.

"Turned around, it becomes AND – the ultimate connector and expander."[15]

Earth anagrams into a heart, the universal symbol for Love, Nature's currency. Another H gives you hearth. The Earth is our hearth and home.

Humus, the dark organic soil produced by rotting animal or vegetable matter, is another earth word rooted in humiliation and humility.

Both mean humbled, but while humiliation implies shame, humility is the sense of being awed by a perceptive shift – a vast difference between the two.

When used in the vocabulary of the purification space, Jacqueline says the term 'heart' moves into the part of you that 'earths' using the six elements to form yourself.

"In that elemental world, you can express as the six elements (that) start to materialize in and through you, because the heart of your being is (about) interconnections and interrelationships between sun and water."[16]

---

15   Airica, 2013
16   Jacqueline, oraclegirl.org 2021

NOTES AND TONES

Mel Gouws, a counselor with psychic abilities, says people tell her their true story just with "the words they use, the patterns and music in their speech."

South African biofield tuner and crystal singing bowl practitioner Wendy Leppard says the pitch of a client's voice tells her more than their language. The voice is the body's metronome and our most potent natural healing instrument.

Wendy listens for harmony and resonance in the tones.

"How clients use their words reveals created limitations through un-helpful mental constructs or images that distort self-perceptions. The word 'want,' for example, implies lack and scarcity.

"A sense of something missing distracts from the authentic expression of an unlimited creative Self. Eliminating words like 'should, must, have to, or need' from our vocabulary is how we create more space in our lives to lighten up and play instead of buying into dated mindsets that no longer serve us. Natural therapies can create more ease, elegance, and harmonic flow."

Wendy shifts old patterns and activates the holographic vortexes in the body's electro-magnetic informational biofield. She says toning, singing, or humming helps the body become coherent.

"We are crystalline in structure. Our inner song resounds from every cell in our bodies.

"We use our voices and sounds with curiosity, listening, and attuning to sense, feel, hear and see vibrations, frequency, and realign energy beyond the conscious mind.

"The more we shift the lens of our perception and focus inward, the more we remember what we are – notes in Nature's orchestra.

"As the Earth transforms and evolves to a higher octave, we too can evolve holographically.

"Vibration is the key. The fastest way to change resonance is to hum, sing, dance, stretch, chant, run, jump, anything that causes a different vibration.

"Notice any response within. Move intuitively from there. Suspend judgment of yourselves, others, and situations to quieten confusion in the brain."

Conscious creation is the awareness we create our realities with our energies and convictions underlying our thoughts and perceptions. Your world is a reflection of your mind.

You can have any experience on Earth within your spectrum of frequencies, but the actual setting is locked, Jacqueline says. "While positive emotions make you feel better and improve your life, a frequency setting can only occur with a physical, spiritual, emotional, or mental merging with anyone who resonates with the new bandwidth.

"One world falls away, and another comes into view. A change of frequency setting happens at particular points in history that send ripples across universes and recalibrate all existences."

"Personal instructions within our physical bodies enable this change in frequency and automatically upgrade as we emerge from the pupa of slave-self perceptions."

I say bring it on. Queens fluent in the universal language of vibration can smash through corporate jargon and word-control parameters.

Embracing Nature's wisdom and your sovereign strength is how you seize the reigns.

Eight Ways To Speak To Power:

1. **CHOOSE YOUR MIRRORS WISELY** *when it comes to expressing yourself.*

2. **LEVEL UP YOUR LEXICON.** *Expand your vocabulary. Become aware of the cognitive vibration attached to the words you choose to express.*

3. **IMMERSE YOURSELF IN SILENCE.** *Allow the currencies of courage and care to convey answers to you. Any thought spoken out aloud will accelerate its velocity.*

4. **WRITE AFFIRMATIONS:** *Make them rhyme for resonance and easier recall.*

5. **MASTER THE PAUSE** *for more honest conversational cargo. Learn to slow down the carousel of thoughts in any situation.*

6. **REFRAME AND RELAX:** *Nature is your only solution. Allow Her to reboot and transmute the slave-self identity experiencing the problem.*

7. **RESEARCH SOMETHING RANDOM.** *Algorithms curate most of what you see online. AI shapes your worldview and traps you in a small perceptual bubble to confirm all your biases.*

8. **ASK YOURSELF WHAT CURRENCY YOU CAN GENERATE.** *Your words cause a ripple effect. Can you find buoyancy in waves of care? Every thought held with conviction comes into being.*

Quick Fixes

Shrug off that pesky, angst-amped identity with this three-minute pick-me-up. Best done barefoot on the ground.

1. **BREATHE IN AS DEEPLY AS YOU CAN.** *Hold it and mentally confront the source of your angst for seven seconds. Bend forward. As you do, express the word 'undo' as you expel all the air from your lungs. Do this until you feel calmer.*

2. **STAND STILL,** *place your hand over your heart and breathe through your nose. With eyes closed, give thanks for whatever gladdens your heart. Know that whatever you relinquish to Nature can be eradicated, transmuted, and regenerated in the tinkle of a merry laugh and withdrawal of (conscious or sub-conscious) consent.*

3. **LISTEN TO SOLFEGGIO FREQUENCIES.**

4. **FOCUS ON WHAT YOU'RE DOING.** *Mindfulness can move you from fear to faith. Concentrate on each body part without letting your mind wander. List five things you can see, four you can hear, three you can touch, two you can smell, and one you can taste. Run cold water over your wrists, mentally shine up your aura, and you're good to go.*

THROAT CONGESTION:
Swallowing your words or suppressing your voice can manifest in throat congestion. Pause before speaking to express yourself clearly with authenticity. Drink warm water with mint, honey, or both. Hum or even scream into a pillow if you need to release emotion, says Wendy Leppard, who also recommends inversions – 'even just a forward bend to get your head lower than your heart, so the blood flows differently."

CHAPTER 9

AIR QUEEN

"Music gives color to the air of the moment."
– KARL LAGERFELD

A ir is my element. I am heir to it all. When I think about Gaia the Earth, Uranos the Sky, great grandmother Themis, I feel free – a unique note within an oceanic sonic symphony.

My husband Zeus swallowed his first wife, Metis. Me, tis me!

Did I, Themis, digest and assimilate Metis to grow more robust in our multidimensionality? Was she a part of, or apart from, me? See how confusing words can be.

The Air Queen wields a sword in most Tarot decks. I use mine to sever whatever colonists stole from nature to create the slavish me.

Was I once a monkey? Simian anagrams to I is man. Is that a coded clue? If I follow the mo(o)ney, will I find the moon key?

Dark clouds park on my mind's perimeter like limousines at a politician's funeral. Let them lurk. The truth will reign despite the misty drizzle of false histories obfuscating our stories.

HEIR TO REALITY

It is in the Air that thoughts become things. Only Air can rise to the summits required to elucidate the mysteries that might not otherwise be possible.

I'm on a quest. A quest I on! Invisibility is my superpower. I can go where I want, do what I want. Nobody stops me if nobody sees me. Personalities shift like the wind between the stillness and the action – gentle breezes here, raging hurricanes there.

I listen in the answering silence. Is everyone I meet en route another version of me? And who knew there would be so many?

Multitudes of identities emerge with every rise and fall of my breath. All are real. None are me. Some rant about injustice; others eat humble pie with coffee. All seek my company.

These houseguest frequencies grew heavy. They stomped across my biofield and entered my chambers with nary a knock.

Once, they enthralled – these hungry ghosts seeking purification through me. But they took without giving and bored me rigid with their tales of woe. They had to go.

When their fearful dependencies started determining events on my timeline, I booted them out and yanked up the drawbridge. Chop. Chop. A swish of my sword. Away they went.

Forgive the poetic license. My sword is proverbial. I stepped back and let nature's fiery glare loosen my grip on their reality. Their business no longer concerned me.

With a farewell flap of my hankie and airblown kisses, their aspects dispersed like ashes in a gale, even as more kept coming.

A queen does not comply. She sees the lie between the 'e' and the 'f' in the valued currency of her belief.

Merging with the frequency of integrity far above nebulous corporate promises vying for her attention, she doesn't lower her vibe for anyone. Her connection to Source is her individuality.

Breathe in. Breathe out. But wait. Breathing unencumbered in a public place constitutes a crime, remember. Keep your nose covered. Obey. Comply. Or what? *Die?* Hah! Death holds no fear for me!

You never know when another pesky fear merchant from the slave-self setting will pop up.

That's why springcleaning, or purification if you prefer, is ongoing. I knew too much of what *they* wanted me to know. Infotainment, or what passes for media, first fêtes, shocks, then persecutes us into obedience.

Independence sounds like In Deep And Dense.

Prisoners serve sentences. Frequencies of phonetic confusion and CGI fakery confine us from within. Compliance thickens the self-imposed walls around our body cells.

The constant repetition of vibratory tones 'catapults the propaganda,' as George Bush once put it, to lock us in. We jail ourselves.

Ah, but no saccharine bombardment of doom merchandise, triggering soundbite or salient song, can confine a sovereign soul for long. When you unveil the mystery, alchemy, and origins of etymology, hear the silent interchange of letters, see how one four-letter word contains many – live, veil, evil, and vile, for example – you form 'knew sentiences.'

You learn the double-edged sword of suppression can hide the truth and magnify the lie via false censorship and other nefarious means.

My royal white-gloved particle-wave shortcircuits all jagged frequencies, rebuffs their ridiculous rules and assertions with zinging velocity. Light laughter shreds the flimsy fabric of their fascist intentions. How absurd they are. What a wheeze!

Craven images from former lives disperse like smoke rings through an air vent.

Whirlwind portals suck them into a transmutational memory hole: a life of travel and song with so much debris.

So long, farewell, *Auf Wiedersehen.* All gone. The relief feels palpable. What took me so long?

I sharpened the blades of reason and discernment, cut through a forest of confusing corporate concepts, and laid bare my path.

I retrieved the embedded treasure box from the lake bed of my petrified rage to shake out ancestral artifacts and burned them to ash with my fiery thoughts.

Cue the delighted cackle of the crone whose power is mighty indeed!

My body is an antenna tuned to sound and frequency. Telepathy and precognition now come naturally to me. My blindfold allowed me to perceive the hidden and unseen.

My multidimensional Self kissed me awake from a corporate dream, not in a rapey Sleeping Beauty way, but by inspiring a narrative re-write from ridiculous restriction into an expansive magical infinity of possibilities.

FAST TRAIN TO SOVEREIGNTY

An electro-magnetic track system for infinite trains or flights of fancy speeds you either to Sovereignty, Synchronicity, or Scarcity, depending on the departure station and carriage you choose.

Depart from Sagacity and Simplicity stations for a serene atmosphere and plush seating. The last train that leaves from Despair is standing room only.

Cool arctic breezes? Lean out of the window, Madame!

Both destinations traverse dark tunnels and vertigo-inducing views, but while one petrifies, the other exhilarates.

Let your baggage go. Lightness is key to creating a more excellent reality. See it as a re-leaf the way a tree does in Spring.

Aboard our thought train, the royal We – Me, Myself, I, Her – enjoy fresh perspectives from luggage racks to first-class carriages. I'm the passenger, driver, and engineer too – who knew?

Of course, we popped into the engine room, but I prefer the dining car with those dinky bottles of spirits. Absinthe of purpose. Djinn and Tonic, anyone?

Having been a First and Business Class flyer in my PC – Pre Covid – life, my preferred seat is in the lap of luxury. Poverty is over-rated; my cats all agree. They enjoy the luxury of lap and remind me it's never too soon for a nap. We like to muse in comfort; we don't do scarcity.

Luxury is a sense of calm within a soothing flow of unhurried moments. You risk leaping on the wrong train when you rush to your destination.

To slow down is to surmount potential obstacles. Give yourself time to seek transparency or discern who wants what. If anything comes at me too fast, I step back from the platform and let it move on. Not my train. Not my station.

I have more than enough time – whatever that is these days – to continue my journey in comfort on the next carriage.

Touch wood – hat tip to the tree spirit – it's what I do. Thank you!

For too many years, I circled the narrative in the inescapable labyrinth of my dreams like a dog chasing its tail – a scribe chasing her tale.

The belief in somewhere else to go drove me until I realized there *was* nowhere to go, no matter where I went. It made perfect sense. Nowhere to go, so *know* where to go.

Quite an admission for a travel hack, I know. The answers smoke out the burning questions.

Where am I going? I am going nowhere. I am 'now here.' Where else is there?

Each journey took me through new points, scales of time, experiences, and wavelengths of comprehension, where I learned to know myself anew.

All car, plane, and train trips led to my sensory interpretation and perceptions of a place. *Moi Toujours!*

If every sojourn led back to myself; if everyone I met was just another variation of me, then whatever I'd hoped to find on all my jaunts and holiday jollies had to be – yep – me again.

Who else? Not just any old me in a new bikini, mind you. (As if.)

No, I was discovering a more upgraded, multidimensional version of Mother Earth ME experiencing reality through my mind-body antenna, sensing rain, sun, or smoke in every uttered word, relishing every nanosecond of being alive.

I was falling in love with myself. Everything I'd ever dreamed of in a relationship came from inside me. What fun!

By merging elemental energies, I could – at least in theory – direct hurricanes from the calm sanctuary of my observation and keep becoming more. Ding! Dong! Bring it *on.*

Fluency in the language of frequencies, sounds, and symbols invites more access to nature's consciousness. She makes it available to all Her children, even when some days feel more expansive than others.

At times I felt like an unwilling passenger on the Ghost Train at Life's Carnival lurching around tracks to confront yet another mocking skeleton. When I peeked behind the scenery to see who was operating the machinery, it felt dark, shadowy, and chilling, neither fun nor fair. That's the problem with the game of life. It demands winners and losers. Real-life, ergo nature, thrives on collaboration, currencies of care, and qualities that defy division.

Not the downloadable Facebook frame variety to virtue signal your compliance as a good, upstanding citizen – even as you urge everyone else into the lunacy of medical tyranny or a war.

I'm talking fluency in the language of energy to recognize familiar patterns in the prevailing narrative and manipulation attempts.

The former frames you as an intellectual zombie.

Nothing dissolves your sovereignty faster than thirsting after the good opinions of others.

Impure motives dilute the distilled essence of integrity, reducing its potency. Whatever you allow through your temple portals will reside in your mind.

If you don't curate your infotainment feeds and keep your thinking independent, somebody else will do it for you. While it's essential to consider all variants of a situation before you hitch your star to the latest wagon of a scientific diktat, when you align with nature's principles, the knowledge you seek will always be there when you need it.

"The purity of every being embodies more deeply when you power up," says Jacqueline.

Springcleaning, simplifying, and purifying keep you regal and sovereign.

AIR

ACTIVATE *the purification pathway. Ask (and allow.)*
Awaken to your divine connection.

IMMERSE *your imagination into your interconnectedness with all things.*

REBOOT, *transmute, and resonate with your inner sun's pure love*
golden frequency.

AIR QUEEN

Decoding magic is her hidden natural power. She unveils, sets alight, and writes
new narratives within an expanding environment of fresh possibilities.

Quiver arrows:
Truth, self-reliance, independence, fairness, intelligence,
objectivity, discernment, skepticism, realism, an air of supreme confidence.
She turns the soil of arcane wisdom to discover new meanings.

Archetype:
Themis, ancient Titan goddess of divine law and order Daughter of Gaia, the
Earth goddess, and Uranus, the sky god, Themis was wife and counselor to Zeus,
plotting with him to cause the Trojan war when he felt the Earth had become
over-populated. She wore a blindfold, weighed the Justice Scales, and shared a
temple with Nemesis, the Greek goddess of retribution.

REFERENCES

Chapter 7 Air Waves

(n.d.). Medical News Today. Armitage, H. (2018). Sound research. Retrieved from Standford Medicine: https://stanmed.stanford.edu/listening/innovations-helping-harness-sound-acoustics-healing.html

Bonaparte, N. (n.d.). Napoléon Bonaparte Quotes . Retrieved from GoodReads

Boothby, S. (2017, April 13). Does Music Affect Your Mood?

Retrieved from healthline.com/: https://www.healthline.com/health-news/mental-listening-to-music-lifts-or-reinforces-mood-051713

Geere, D. (2011, April 7). The colours of noise. Retrieved from Wired dot com:

Hess, P. (n.d.). Peter Hess Academy. Retrieved from https://www.peterhessacademyusa.com/

Hungerford, D. (2019). Music and Health: Looking at the Blood. Retrieved from Healing Frequencies music dot com: healingfrequenciesmusic.com/music-and-health-looking-at-the-blood/

John, E. (n.d.). Brainy Quotes Elton John. Retrieved from Brainy Quotes:

Karim, D. I. (n.d.). Introduction to Biogeometry. Retrieved from biogeometry.ca: https://www.biogeometry.ca/introduction-to-biogeometry

Leonard G. Horowitz, D. M. (n.d.). Musical cult control:

Retrieved from: https://www.ninefornews.nl/wp-content/uploads/2013/12/muziek-horowitz.pdf

Lipton, B. (2014, June 12). Good Vibrations. BruceLipton.com/good-vibrations. MacMillan, A. (2017, March 8).

The Sound of 'Pink Noise' Improves Sleep and Memory. Retrieved from time.com/

McKusick, E. D. (2019, October 18). Discovering the Biofield Anatomy. McKusick, E. D. (n.d.).

The Books. Retrieved from biofieldtuning.com/the-books

McTaggart, L. (2003, March 31). The Field. Retrieved from Lynne McTaggart: lynnemctaggart.com/

Melanie Braun, M. M. (n.d.). Exploring the Efficacy of Vowel Intonations.

Robin Richman, R. (1969). "An Infinity of Jimis," Life Magazine.

Shore, P. (2014, May). Sanctuaries, Gateways: The Sonic Spaces of Curative and Palliative Music in Medieval Cloister and Infirmary.

Retrieved from Ars Medica: https://www.academia.edu

References

Chapter 8 Air Vents

References Airica, L. (2013, April 15). Distinguished English Linguist: Writing English — And Jumping to Some New Conclusions.

Retrieved from Latina Lista: http://latinalista.com

Bishop, T. (2021, December 2). Reality check: Microsoft, David Bowie, Bill Gates, and a creepy video game called 'Omikron.'

Retrieved from GeekWire: https://www.geekwire.com

Braun, M. (n.d.). Exploring the efficacy of vowel intonations.

Britannica. (n.d.). Logos philosophy and theology. Retrieved from Britannica.com:

Sources and limitations of ancient and modern knowledge. Retrieved from Britannica dot com:

Comity: Retrieved from Lexico: https://www.lexico.com/en/definition/comity

Oraclegirl.org (2021). Retrieved from Oracle Girl: https://www.oraclegirl.org/library Audio file "Track of the month 4' (Dec13).

Last, C. (2014, December 26). Commerce - Law of the Sea. Retrieved from YouTube:

Mina, R. (n.d.). The Influence of the Ancient Egyptian Language on the European Languages. Retrieved from Academia Edu: https://www.academia.edu/4177204/The_Influence_of_the_Ancient_Egyptian_Language_on_the_European_Languages

Oakie42, J. (2022, January 25). Twitter. twitter.com/oakiejs/status/1486008251820830723?s=27

Orlandi, R. (2018, August 6). "I Miss My Liver." Nonmedical Sources in the History of Hepatocentrism.

Retrieved from NCBI: https://www.ncbi.nlm.nih.gov/pmc/articles/PMC6078213/

Twyman, T. (n.d.). Welcome to the unveiling (part 1). Retrieved from the aeon eye: https://theaeon-eye.com/tag/tracy-twyman/

Wiktionary. (n.d.). Smart. Retrieved from Wiktionary:

Abracadabra. Retrieved from World Wide Words: https://www.worldwidewords.org

SECTION IV

EARTH

Earth enables the vibratory thought forms in your toroidal electromagnetic fields to materialize and anchor you in density. Nodes form and individuate in Nature according to your relationship with the other five elements.

Earth's ever-changing consciousness causes our bodies to shed redundant ways of being and morph new biological contours.

CHAPTER 10

EARTH AWARENESS

"Some trees have lived for thousands of years.
They get along, develop sophisticated relationships and listen.
Trees are attuned. Attunement is something
we all need too."
– DR. SUZANNE SIMARD

I love the bush. To explore sub-Saharan Africa's untrammeled savannas on foot before sunrise is to unveil all manner of treasures, from emerald scarabs glittering in rhino middens to ruby red Fairy Crassula.

Wild aniseed scents the cool air as the day chortles to life. Marvel at colonies of red-billed buffalo weaver twig nests divided into separate lodges. The polyamorous male – tantric maven of the avian world – takes up to three minutes to mate with each female in his harem, compared with the mere seconds of other birds.

He's even evolved a false penis. Oh my, the stuff Mother Nature dreams up! Everything has a purpose. Nothing goes to waste. Hyenas – and vultures – eat predator leftovers to clean up the bush.

Leopard tortoises chomp calcium-rich hyena dung to harden their shells. Eagles negotiate thermals above dry undulating ripples of whistling thorn and riverine forest, depicting freedom in a way no artist could.

The Acacia's thorny prospects

The Acacia, ancient Tree of Life, produces DiMethylTryptamine, a psychedelic compound that occurs naturally in human and animal brains.

It's the reason cognitive psychology professor Benny Shanon from the Hebrew University of Jerusalem says Moses must have been high when he encountered the burning Acacia bush and heard God speaking to him.[1]

With its branched, tree-like appearance, the arbor vitae (Tree of Life in Latin), located deep in both cerebellar hemispheres of our brain, regulates hand-eye coordination and conveys sensory information to and from the cerebellum.[2]

Acacia trees in the wild African matrix share their struggles, death-defying dramas, and complicated relationship issues in a voltage-based signaling system.[3]

The fire-resistant Knob Thorn (*Acacia nigrescens*) makes sugary protein treats to feed and enslave the ants who guard it.

The Acacia's hardwood protects it from termites but not elephants that often strip the trunks, feed on the bark, and decimate the grove.

I can't help wondering if the elephants enjoy a high from the bark. Might it be related to their excellent memory?

A thicket of Umbrella Thorn (*Acacia tortillus*) emits distress signals in the form of ethylene gas to warn neighboring acacias to step up tannin production to fend off herbivorous predators.

Tannin toxicity kills kudu in confined spaces and can inhibit a giraffe's ability to digest food, which leads to poor condition and weaker calves that are more likely to succumb to lion predation.[4]

---

1   Shanon, 2016
2   Wikipedia, n.d.
3   Kinzler, 2018
4   Jstor, n.d.

Having evolved with acacias, animals know trees talk to each other. That's why giraffe browse into the wind before the warning gas can reach the other trees. A giraffe eats 30 kg a day of Acacia leaves and twigs, but sadly poaching and shrinking habitats have wiped out 40 percent of the population in just 30 years.

These gentle giants are losing their beloved acacia trees to human settlements, agricultural activities, and increased construction of roads.[5]

Drastic long-term solutions can stave off their extinction, but we need to wake up fast. Ethnobotanist Dr. Dennis McKenna warns that if we don't act by 2040 – "or just get out of the way and let the Earth heal" – it will be too late, and large areas will become uninhabitable.

"Earth should be a garden. Photosynthesis is the answer. We all need to partner up with the biosphere, grow more plants, and take steps to avert this impending disaster. Nothing is more critical right now. That's the deal.

"We don't have the luxury of evolution. We have to identify what we can do to become true symbiotic partners, rather than dominators, to bring us back into alignment."[6]

Out on a limb

The oak – associated with Zeus and Thor – is the most prone to lightning strikes of all trees.

My favorite childhood climbing tree was an oak. The chattering squirrels and magical folk in Enid Blyton's *Magic Faraway Tree* series mesmerized me. I loved to pretend the woods of Hilton in KwaZulu-Natal, where I grew up, were enchanted.

After reading forest ecologist Dr. Suzanne Simard's memoir, *Finding the Mother Tree: Discovering the Wisdom of the Forest*, I realized I wasn't that far off the mark.[7]

Dr. Simard didn't just talk to the trees. She listened.

---

5   Basu, 2017
6   YouTube, 2021
7   Simard, 2021

Exploring the Canadian wilderness near British Columbia's Monashee Mountains throughout her childhood, Dr. Simard instinctively experienced the forest and all its firs, ferns, and fairy bells – "nature in the raw." – as being founded on love and cooperation.

While Western Canada's Aboriginal people's language describes the connection between trees and humanity, Dr. Simard's work shows that trees can recognize us.

The scientific journal Nature featured Dr. Simard's work on its cover in 1997.

Years later, her ground-breaking findings validated her instincts that love had shaped the beauty of the forests of her youth. Scientifically verifying the sentience and intelligence of forest communities, Dr. Simard uprooted redundant, ecologically unsound, and self-defeating forest management fallacies and changed the way the world sees trees.

Thanks to her rigorous research, we know trees communicate, co-operate, exchange nutrients, recognize kin, thrive in diverse communities, make decisions, learn, remember and weed out undesirable characters.

The challenges Dr. Simard faced might have defeated a lesser woman – the tragic death of her rodeo-rider brother, the break-up of her marriage, and breast cancer, to name a few.

And, like any tall tree, the forest ecology professor at the University of British Columbia caught a lot of wind. Colleagues threw shade at her evidence that cooperation was as key as competition in evolution. Her exhumation of a carcass of reigning forest practice inadequacies threatened vested interests. Neighborly reciprocity, healing capacity, and forest wisdom concepts challenged prevailing profit-driven policies of destroying biodiversity in exchange for a single desirable species.

Encompassing the coastal forests of North America to the Arctic, Dr. Simard's research includes the discoveries of the Wood Wide Web and the Mother Tree.

THE WOOD WIDE WEB

The discovery of the underground neural network connecting multiple tree species via roots and fungal filaments to exchange carbon nutrients, water, and information, upended the dominant scientific narrative of competition being the primary forest-shaping force.

Trees and neighboring shrubs exchange phosphorus and nitrogen for carbon-rich sugars.

Branching fungal mycorrhizas – "brilliant as a Persian rug" – act as intermediaries. This sharing is reciprocal.

The rich supply the poor. Trees send carbon based on the degree to which they are shading other trees with seasonal shifts in the resource distribution.

Trees learn from this information to adjust their behaviors to increase growth strategizing, problem-solving, and decision-making.

Trees perceive each other and transmit information to and from each other via fungal links.

The communication molecules transmitted through the network are similar to neurotransmitters in biological neural networks (our brains).

MOTHER TREES:

The oldest trees not only recognize their seedling kin within their fungal web but "mother their children" by sending them sugars, water, nutrients, and information to help them survive. They:

* *Pool resources to protect against infection.*

* *Absorb animal nutrients they transmit to neighbors to fertilize the forest.*

* *Sense nearby plants and animals and warn each other when hungry insects or animals advance. Douglas firs infested with western spruce budworm (Choristoneura occidentalis) warn pines via the Wood Wide Web to produce defense enzymes.*

159

- *Some studies even suggest plant roots grow toward the sound of running water and that certain flowering plants sweeten their nectar when they detect a bee's wing beats.*

- *Know when they're infected and produce an instantaneous biochemical response.*

- *Tap water deep in the soil and send it to neighboring plants and seedlings during times of drought. Resources flow from the oldest and biggest trees to the youngest and smallest.*

- *Sick or dying Mother Trees transmit energy, information, and wisdom to the next generation. Seedlings store the memory in their roots and growth rings.*

Dr. Simard continues to "give back what forests have given to me, a spirit, a wholeness, a reason to be" and shares her discoveries through TED Talks and the Mother Tree Project she founded.[8]

Mycorrhizal networks prevail wherever life exists. If you love walking in Nature, you'll know that.

Dr. McKenna says while there are many ways to communicate with plants, psychedelics, "particularly those in the tryptamine family," help us focus on our relationship to the larger community of life.

"Their revelation – their wake-up call to us – is that we have to change everything about our lifestyle and what we think we know. Plants run the show.

"Finally, the scientific community is beginning to acknowledge that plants have consciousness.

"It's nothing like ours, but a genuine way of interfacing with their environment and other plants and organisms in the biosphere. Their language is chemistry. Their behavior is biosynthesis.

"Plants run everything. Being rooted, they meet environmental challenges where they find them, and the sooner we start working in symbiosis with them, the better off we'll be.

---

8   The Mother Tree project, n.d.

"By capturing cosmic energy from the sun and maintaining the balance of greenhouse gases, plants have mastered the biochemical miracle that enables life in the biosphere.

"They have the answers. We don't. Everything that is not photosynthetic is a parasite on the plants."[9]

Jacqueline says we are more akin to trees than we know. "In time, people will discover that humans evolved in tandem with the plants and animals.

"We could say the human is a leaf being, each a single tree in the forest of humanity. An individual leaf is an essential aspect of the same organism among thousands of others.

"It catches the sun, rain, and elements. It moves as an aspect of the same natural processes."

"With each turn of Nature's grow, live, and die – "undo, transmute, and generate" – cycles, we regreen ourselves, the world, and the future."[10]

In Vancouver, Allen Larocque, an ecologist at the University of British Columbia, uncovered an interlinked fish-forest-fungi system.

Trees absorb salmon nitrogen and other nutrients from carcasses left by bears in the forest, then share it through the network. "Soils are active, living places full of bacteria and fungi that act as intermediaries between the salmon and the trees," he says.[11]

In his book *Cosmic Serpent: DNA and the Origins of Knowledge*, Jeremy Narby describes communicating with two massive, fluorescent snakes after taking ayahuasca. (Narby, 1999)

The author anthropologist who lived for two years with the Ashaninca in the Peruvian Amazon, points out that few anthropologists looked into the enigma of how so-called primitive people knew so much about the molecular properties of plants *and the art of combining them.*"

While he initially wrote off as "irrational superstitions," the Ashinca's description of plants and animals "as intelligent beings with personalities that communicated with humans in visions and dreams," he "saw the

---

9   YouTube, 2021
10   Jacqueline, oraclegirl.org
11   Larocque, n.d.

arrogance of my worldview" after drinking Ayahuasca, "the television of the forest," at the behest of a shaman.

He describes in *The Mind of Plants: Narratives of Vegal Intelligence*, edited by John C Ryan, Patricia Vieira, and Monica Gagliano, working with cannabis as a "plant editor" that allowed him to reread his words with detachment in the writing process [12]

Shamans will tell you plants – like the sun – have a song. We all sing the body electric!

PLANT ACOUSTICS

The evolutionary ecologist Dr. Monica Gagliano whose daring and imaginative research pioneered the field of plant bioacoustics, proved the shamans correct when she showed roots emitted a sound inaudible to humans at a frequency of 220 Hertz to communicate.

By having the courage to defy the confines of scientific dictates, the author, seer, provocateur, research fellow, and a professor at Southern Cross University in Australia achieved the miraculous – bridging the divide between conventional science and the unknown.

It took her a decade, but her willingness to dismantle her scientist identity and be okay with awkwardness and anxiety struck gold.

"I didn't know how to do my work from within a prescribed box that felt too tight.

"The Colonial way of doing science – taking plants from their environments, giving them Latin names that described nothing – made no sense.

"You don't have to know a plant's name to connect to it.

"Killing things in the service of others justifies violence. If you move humans into different conditions, they will not be the same.

Intelligent, communicative beings, plants too, learn, choose, and remember things.

"What does putting them in a lab and ignoring their properties achieve?"

---

12   Ryan, 2021

Dr. Gagliano lived with anxiety for a decade, "staying within the game," but her question to the plants burned inside her: "How do I create a setting to allow you, the plant, to show yourself?"

As they do for so many who seek their counsel, plants came to her rescue.

One angst-ridden day lying on the ground in a forest of swaying pines, she heard their message in the soft sibilance of their whispering: 'Be in the wind, be flexible. Otherwise, you will break.'

"Another plant told me anxiety meant I was at the edge of my box. I needed to break free.

"I had to go from science and reconnect within Nature's web as the human. Anxiety's job was to nudge me into moving.

"Now, I break down those barriers as soon as I bump against them. The message of flexibility from the pines reminds me to feel comfortable being between places of knowledge. Tension is essential to creation, moving, connecting, and living."

Tension holds the flexible suspension bridge Dr. Gagliano built to enable seekers to traverse the controlled environment of science on one side and the unknown on the other.

So she has fulfilled her intention.

"I always wish to feel in tension," she says. "I'm comfortable with messiness, thanks to my training in field ecology training. Learning is complex and unresolved.

"Ecologists want to know the bigger why. They don't care so much about where a sample originated. Clean data is not the field ecology motivation.

"Workers in the sanitized space of a laboratory are primarily biologists wanting to know details and the mechanics of how something works.

"I ended up in the lab because of my questions, but you cannot extract something, isolate, dissect it, and expect big-picture knowledge.

"The lab was never my place. It was just the first section of the bridge I needed to build. What the bridge holds together and who will walk on it interests me more."

Like Dr. Simard, Dr. Gagliano's immense contributions to Plant Cognitive Ecology 'upset' some of her more traditionally-minded colleagues. Who cares? Her version of science is so much more badass and accessible to all.

"The Nature I observe is more significant. In searching everywhere, we seek ourselves. We let others show us who they are and not who we want them to be. The aspect of play in our practices is crucial – and with its limitations, science forgets that.

"Let's transcend words. Let's experience Nature through the arts and music. Reciprocity, compromise, awareness, and presence are essential ingredients of any relationship.

Adds Dr. Gagliano, "It's the same with plants. You can interact with them in your unique way."[13]

Talking to the Trees

Australian "psychic-medium, artist, truth seeker, spiritual warrior, and cosmic traveler," JC Kay's arboreal conversations reveal their supportive purpose.

They've told her telepathically – as a "collective part of Nature, a conduit for Earth goddess Gaia" – their purpose is to awaken us, "the sleeping ones, the walking trees."

The message from the trees is this: "All of Nature stands by to support you if you would connect and be one with us! We are here waiting for you to listen.

"Come back to us, to the Earth, to unity. Be brave. Reach deep within you for that spark of creation. You will overcome this great war on all creation."

JC discovered her abilities when she made friends with a tree outside her apartment.

"First, the tree said, 'now we are holding hands.' I felt the tree was she, although she said 'binary' – which turned out to be true."

"Energetically, the tree asked me to remind humanity of our connection to each other and Nature. I resonated with the role."

---

13   Gagliano, 2022

JC does not talk to "an entity." Her Higher Self receives and unveils messages. Conversations float into her head as the tree communicates "like many as one in a distant monotone."

"They function as collective antennae, part of a connected consciousness that includes the smallest grass blade.

"Like us, trees have been contained, poisoned, manicured, and forced into cramped containers.

"They enjoy the sun and find the frost hard on them in winter.

"They invite us to recharge by grounding ourselves in the Earth.

"Mother Earth transmutes all of this matrix crumbling around us, exposing the organic, the truth, and the world that covered up the lies."

An abridged version communique from the trees to JC Kay reminds us: "We are one with you, and our knowing traverses all planes and territories.

"There are layers beneath the surface of this Earth, either accessed physically or from a higher dimension.

"We connect in the root systems and the frequencies carried across time and space.

"(There is) a cluster of connected 'crystal cities spread across this sacred brown land' – Australia – that activate and emit a charge when the 'Originals who live on the surface' sing into the songlines."

"The trees remind us we, humanity, were given the tools countless times, yet we ignore them and disconnect from the truth, from Earth, from Gaia.

"You are part of Gaia, one with God and creation. What distracts you is anti-creation – the opposite of creation.

"It is an energy and a rogue technology – worse than the one that created the cataclysm of Atlantis.

"The technology holds a parasitic frequency that wishes to harness your greatness.

"You must not be distracted. Push through. Seek your truth and knowing. We, the standing ones, urge you, the walking trees, to call upon your truth.

"Do not be distracted by toxic thoughts, ideals, and technology. "We ask you to rise into your greatness and recharge with us.

"The answers are here in us. We have given you the answers time and again.

"The pine tree, the fallen bark, the rotting leaves all gave you answers to heal.

"And you reject us. You believe you are more significant than Nature. Release your pressure and anxiety.

"Lean against a tree, ground yourself. Feel that pull to clear yourself of all that is unnatural. We are here to heal you.

"We stand strong and tall. Our branches, trunks, and leaves sway in the wind.

"We are rooted in great Gaia, connected – not once are we corrupted. We are here waiting for you all to listen.

"You will overcome this great war on all creation.

"We are counting on you. We urge you to feel your connection to God. They (the dark ones) wish to disconnect you, but we want to remind you that you are God's most incredible creation.

"Nothing to be done, but to still your heart and know – YOU HAVE WON."

JC, who dowses with a pendulum to 'verify' her arboreal messages, says we can all communicate with trees.

"The more your relationship develops with a tree, the better your communication will be."[14]

THE TREES TALK BACK

- *Go back to your roots.*
- *Answers lie in creation and Nature.*
- *Be grounded and know the truth.*
- *Reconnect to Nature and your inner self.*
- *Mourn the loss of the old but rejoice in the new.*
- *Go within.*
- *Create anew from the ashes of the old.*
- *Everything not of Nature is corrupted and false.*
- *Tap in to feel the Earth's heartbeats*

---

14   Kay, n.d.

- When you become fluent in the first language of energy, you feel the truth.
- The body knows the difference between truth and lies.
- A new Earth is rising. The old one is waning.

7 PLANT PROPERTIES

1. Plants have a mind and can transmit knowledge to humans.
2. There is no division between mind and body in plants.
3. Plants are masters of chemistry. It's how they communicate.
4. Trees emit chemical, hormonal, and electrical pulses, and so do we.
5. Communication networks in all biospheres regulate the ecosystem to maintain equilibrium.
6. Trees can detect scents through their leaves and have a sense of taste.
7. Trees can feel and experience something analogous to pain, sending electrical signals like wounded human tissue when cut.

Four Earth Affirmations:

1. I create whatever I wish to exist
2. I find common ground with everything around me.
3. I am here now and free to honor all of Earth's energy
4. My strength is my deep connection with the sun, soil, and sky.

CHAPTER 11

SOLID GROUNDING

"Going barefoot is the gentlest way of walking and can symbolize a way of living - that has the lightest impact, removing the barrier between us and nature."
– ADELE COOMBS, BAREFOOT DREAMING

Back pain is the leading cause of disability worldwide. If, as Phyllis Diller once quipped, your back goes out more than you do – as it does in 80% of people's lives – then moving forward might feel difficult. Most back pain diminishes on its own, but in the meantime, you might want to figure out for yourself what eases or worsens the pain.

Most of us can treat our back pain at home, preferably after a few consultations with a professional to rule out inflammatory arthritis, infection, fracture, or cancer as a cause.[1]

Experiment with a gentle forward bend or a couple of yoga moves.

---

1   American Chiropractic Association, 2022

My favorite way to alleviate discomfort is to lie on the floor with a book under my head for support, a heated pad on the sore area, and my legs propped against a wall or closed door for 20 to 30 minutes.

The relief is immediate. I do this every morning now. It's also an excellent position for meditating or listening to music.

THE ALEXANDER TECHNIQUE

The Alexander Technique, a psychophysical process, can help you function more efficiently for long-term improvement.

Dubbed the Westerner's Zen, Hollywood actors Juliette Binoche and Annette Bening swear by it. Ms. Binoche described it as "a way to transform stress to joy," while Ms. Bening said: "Good acting is revealing yourself. If your body is free, your mind is free.

"The (Alexander Technique) will create new habits (to) serve you well through aging."[2]

South African actress and Alexander Technique teacher Jana Cilliers says: What we get up to – our reaction to stimuli – can often feel right no matter how wrong or unsatisfactory it is.

"We impact the incorrect use of our bodies from childhood with the subconscious imitation of parents, teachers, and leaders, so the Technique is a learning process of undoing or freeing bad postural habits.

"Pulling the head back, pushing it forward, stiffening the shoulders, contracting and hollowing the back, collapsing the rib cage, tilting the pelvis forward, and gasping for breath are examples of improper use.

"We remain unconscious of these habits until significant strain and discomfort strike. Only then do we stop in our tracks and reach for palliative measures.

"Frozen shoulders, stiff necks, writer's cramp, back pain, heart flutters, arthritis, and depression are all symptoms of body misuse.

"Being a gym bunny or exercise devotee can do more harm because you intensify and worsen ongoing bad physical habits.

"Osteopaths and chiropractors may iron out kinks, but until you relearn the proper use of your body, the aches and pains will return."

---

2   Complete Guide to the Alexander Technique, n.d.

Your thoughts are as important as the correct use of your posture.

The trick is to pause and be willing to change your mental and physical aspects for the better.

"Messages of release and direction within the body take time," says Ms. Cilliers. "Teacher and learner work towards eliminating the wrong posture and accompanying thought waves to allow the correct pattern to reassert itself.

"Reaching for a result without living more consciously to achieve it is our biggest stumbling block. Since we function as a whole, we can only change as a whole.

"Erroneous patterns and stimuli responses take root in our nervous system and muscle tone.

"Fixed opinions and emotional reactions plague us as much as physical tensions. To see the proper use of the body, observe toddlers who have not yet learned to tense their movements."

When his voice and stage presence began to fail, Frederick Matthias Alexander, an Australian actor, used mirrors to study his actions. While his kinesthetic sense believed his posture was correct, the mirror revealed his tendency to pull his head back and down, depress his larynx, gasp for air, and shorten his stature when speaking. Excess neck tension was causing his problems.

He corrected his head, neck, and back relationship to create the best conditions for speech – the primary control for optimal body functioning – but was shocked to notice he continued to misuse his body when speaking.

The idea of oration alone made him follow his old habit over his new intention. He concluded his sensory mechanism was false.

He decided to pause before speaking. That way, he could direct his neck to be free to allow his head to go "forward and up so his back could lengthen and widen."

Inhibition and direction are the cornerstones of the Alexander Technique. Prohibiting the building up of undue tension enables you to "respond to stimuli with calm and conscious volition, and ... enjoy freedom in thought and action."

The spinal cord's 31 nerve pairs and support cells have distinct central nervous system roles but depend on each other to accomplish their tasks.

A combination of awareness and powerful intention can facilitate a natural flow from the brain to correct spinal alignment with the neck, head, and brainstem.

As Alexander changed his thought patterns, noting subsequent physical changes, he got the best out of his voice, and his ailments vanished.

"The way we think lies at the heart of how we act. And the way we act is the primary cause of our physical woes or wellness," he said.

When triggered, your movements reveal whether your actions are impulsive or considered. Zanna uses the Alexander Technique to bring "the structure of my being" into natural alignment.

"I love how my energy flows when I correct my posture. We experience the world through our bodies, so the more we connect with them, the better our emotional health and sense of freedom.

"Movement is beneficial, but most of us learn to function in a way that misuses the body. We bend from the spine instead of our hinges – our hips, knees, and ankles.

"Sitting at your computer with hunched shoulders, a bent spine, and a tight neck compresses your nerves and energy flow.

"Alexander's work enables me to uncover and stop harmful habits. My mind and body are one unit. I can affirm qualities in the alignment between my neck, head, and spine to heal my posture. Like anything that honors the miracle of your body in a gentle, organic way, the process takes time. When trauma dictates how you see yourself, the Alexander Technique can give you the backbone to heal painful situations.

"Start with your mind – your thoughts about what you believe yourself to be. When you shed everything you are not, you become aware of your true, magnificent essence."

Three Tenets of the Alexander Technique

1. **THE SINGLE MIND-BODY UNIT**
   Mastering the correct movements allows us to change our self-image, control our impulses, improve coordination, and surpass psychological assumptions.

   "You translate everything – physical, mental, or spiritual into muscular tension."
   – FM ALEXANDER, (1869-1955)

2. **KINESTHETIC DEBAUCHERY**
   Unreliable sensory appreciation explains why you may feel like you're doing something you're not.

   "Sensory appreciation conditions conception; you can't know a thing by a wrong instrument. You are not making decisions; you are doing what you feel to be right kinaesthetically. Trying emphasizes what we know already."
   – FM ALEXANDER

3. **NATURAL POISE**
   Uncover harmful bad habits that prevent you from experiencing your natural, healthy correct posture. Use verbal direction or auto-suggestion to achieve balance. Natural poise is our birthright. Reclaim this instinct.

   "If you stop doing the wrong thing, the right thing will do itself."
   – FM ALEXANDER

173

COME HELL OR HIGH HEELS

Why do we use 'downtrodden' and 'well-heeled' to describe poor or wealthy people?

If you've ever tottered about in stupid, strappy stilettos, you'll understand there's no bigger oxymoron than well-heeled.

Heels/heals – another homonym with opposite meanings. Heel heights cause harm.

There must be a special place in hell for footwear designers and whichever misogynist coined the phrase 'women in sensible shoes' to describe unfeminine harridans.

The entertainment industry's portrayal of a sexy woman is a drag artist's fantasy.

They feign camp horror at the sight of unpolished toenails, auxiliary hair, or anything natural.

They hate real women, so they trick you into believing "longer-looking legs" make you more attractive to men.

Your reward for hobbling about like a spavined old nag in pursuit of same?

Think chewed cocktail sausages for toes, bunions, carbuncles, weak arches, and hammer-toed foot deformities. More fool you for believing them, or that love has anything to do with the length of your legs.

How fast do you think you could run in heels?

The tilting and joint adjustments required to keep the body erect in heels involve ankles, knees, hips, spine, head, ligaments, joints, muscles, tendons, and internal alterations. These, in turn, lead to fatigue, leg, back, and shoulder aches.

Postural adaptation is required even for low heels. The synthetic rubber sole ungrounds us and makes natural gait biomechanically impossible for any shoe-wearer. Take your shoes off already!

The Earth Queen needs no heels to walk tall. Bare feet require no 'compensatory wedge angles' since the body weight is shared equally between the heel and ball at a 180-degree level.

All shoes convert the normal to the abnormal.

The late podiatrist and footwear historian Dr. William Rossi wrote in *Podiatry Management*. No therapy or mechanical device, no matter how precisely designed or expertly applied, can reverse the (wrong) gait."[1]

Worse still, rubber soles insulate you from the Earth, your best source of negative ions that counteract harmful EMFs (electromagnetic frequencies) from our Wi-Fi and home wiring.

Clinton Ober, co-author of *Earthing, The most important health discovery ever?* says our bodies can absorb and emit up to 20 volts of electricity.[2]

Like cables, we need to ground to maintain our systems in a stable electrical environment. Our sole-to-ground connections absorb electrons that lightning spews into the ionosphere.

Earthing rids the body of inflammation, a leading cause of cancer and heart disease, by allowing electrons to coat your red blood cells.

Putting your hands and feet on good soil is one of the best ways to build immunity.

Without a daily barefoot walk on grass, beach, or ground, your tissues absorb more free radicals.

I felt sluggish and slow before I started barefoot walking two decades ago. Within a week of connecting my bare soles with the soil, a sense of vibrancy replaced the lethargy, aches, and pains.

Something else I no longer suffer from is jetlag. The first thing I did to rejuvenate my jetlagged self whenever I flew overseas was to walk barefoot on the grass somewhere.

Walking is my sacred path to freedom. Barefoot, I've traversed sun-dappled forest paths from Hong Kong to Thailand, picked wild berries from European hedges, and watched monkeys in the Victoria Falls rain forest. My immune system has never been more robust.

Grounding, unblocking your flow, and moving fluidly through the conscious manifestation of your life unleashes a sense of childlike joy as you keep stepping into an exciting new timeline.

When my soles touch Earth and the wind fills my lungs, I ground and absorb Nature's golden love frequency. When you realize there is

---

1   D.P.M, n.d.

2   Ober, 2010

no physical existence without our sacred Mother, you understand the inheritance of Earth's inherent power is a gift beyond price.

Her age-old tools of natural magic – the soil, rushing water, trees, grass – await only your touch or intention to create.

FOREST BATHING

Forest bathing is a lyrical name for wandering in the woods. Japanese researchers showed pine forest fragrances elevated levels of Natural Killer or NK cells in the immune system.

Even diffusing phytoncides (cedar essential oils) in a room where people slept caused a significant spike in NK cells.[3]

The Earth's electrically charged negative ions can heal our bodies from the constant bombardment of positive-ion generating electromagnetic fields, cell phones, TV, computers, and 5G that can affect our immune, endocrine, blood, lymph, and nervous systems.

Forests, beaches, and waterfalls emit charges of between 2 500 and 5 000 negative ions. Office environments emit only 70.[4]

Dr. Suzanne Simard believes there's a physiological explanation for the unburdening sensation we experience through Nature.

"When you're walking in the forest, a whole city underfoot includes myriad organisms, including actinomycetes (bacteria) that excrete chemicals that can make us a bit high – there's an aphrodisiac thing going on.

"You know when it rains, and you get that earthy smell? Water gets into the soil, and the bacteria burst – that's what we're smelling."[5]

Richard Louv, who coined the phrase Nature Deficit Disorder to describe people who spend too much time indoors, says: "Time in nature is not leisure time; it's an essential investment in our children's health (and also, by the way, in our own)."[6]

---

3   Li, 2009
4   Warrior29, 2021
5   Simard, 2021
6   Louv, 2016

Rachel and Stephen Kaplan's Attention Restoration Theory (ART) holds that paying attention in stressful environments requires way more effort than it does outdoors.[7]

Hygge Queen Sandra Hogberg of Puyallup, Washington, uses trees to transmute anger or fear. "I place my hands on a tree, give it my negativity with gratitude, and look to its roots for grounding. Nature heals through the divine."

THE BODY'S WISDOM

Your body knows things about you and your surroundings long before your mind catches up.

The mother who awakens and understands her child has died before the painful truth is confirmed; the voice in your head screaming STOP just before you disturb a puffadder you hadn't seen on the path.

Your body lives in the present, receiving and transmitting energy, while your mind is elsewhere or on autopilot. That's how it knows things before you do.

When we stop over-ruling what our bodies are telling us, we can move forward in life with more fluidity. It might be something as simple as disliking certain foods.

Denise Bjorkman had a history of sustained headaches and hated the taste of espresso. Only when a DNA test showed her liver could not metabolize coffee did she make the connection.

"Tuning into my body helped me develop a higher level of self-awareness. My headaches vanished when I stopped drinking coffee because my body's wisdom had spoken."

Thanks to the media and entertainment industries bombarding us with images of what our bodies should look like, too many of us obsess over our cellulite or wobbly thighs that fall short of impossible standards.

The more we tune into and resonate with an unnatural system, the more we allow it to infiltrate our biofields and distort our body signaling. Learn to discern how your body communicates with you. Notice your reaction to anything you hear, see, or read. Dark, false, or harmful

---

7   Ruth, n.d.

information will cause tension in your solar plexus. Your stomach will tighten.

Love-based information leads to a lightness of heart, which transmutes anything not resonating with the love vibration.

Says Dr. Christiane Northrup: "You don't need a system. You are pure love. Take that in. Look in the mirror. Tell yourselves. That's how we very quickly change our biology."[8]

Initially, your body's signaling will combine family patterns, slave-self stuff, and Nature's frequency in various combinations.

To discern which configuration dominates, build a set of experiences based on what your body shows you. Our bodies are energy receivers and transmitters. The more you learn to read and test your body signals, the more you will resonate with the truth.

"The truth resonates differently from lies. When something doesn't feel right, it isn't," says Mel Gouws.

Jacqueline says the gold frequency carried in our blood bridges our cosmic self and material form.

Five ways to rejuvenate:

1. **ALIGN YOUR SPINE:** *Adopting incorrect postural patterns causes you to shrink as you grow older. Better posture and spinal realignment help you regain that "hidden height."*

2. **RECALIBRATE:** *Connect your kinaesthetic sense with your conscious intention to use your mind and body with awareness every day.*

3. **STEP IT UP:** *Walking faster in middle age improves physical and cognitive health. Scientists from Duke University, the University of Otago, and King's College London used an electronic laboratory walkway to analyze the patterns and pace of more than 900 New Zealanders over 40. After testing the effects of speed on cholesterol levels, body mass index (BMI), white blood cell count, and the ability to fight immunity, they found the dawdlers displayed accelerated aging across all the biomarkers*

---

8   Northrup, 2021

and reduced brain volume. Faster walkers achieved more strength and recorded 16 points more in IQ tests. (Rasmussen, 2019)

4. **SWING YOUR ARMS:** *When walking, free your arms to improve stability and reduce the energy required to move the legs.*
    Complex neural connections between your upper and lower limbs enhance the efficiency of your stride pattern. (Carey, n.d.)

5. **ADD SOMETHING TO YOUR LIFE:** *It sounds counter-intuitive, but do something extra when you feel overwhelmed.*
    Here's how four Hygge Queens added something extra to their lives.
    "I added relaxation to my routine and learned to use my body to create at that moment. Reality bends around me when I listen to my essential core," says Scottish artist Caroline Morris.
    Reiki Practitioner and clairvoyant Mel Gouws added art to bring peace and soul flow to her life. "So many people say, 'Oh, I could never do art.' I say try. It is so cathartic and healing."
    Author-artist Donna White added poetry. "I wake up around 3 am with one of the lines in my head. Then I follow the flow of consciousness to complete the rest. Writing poetry and rhymes soothes me."
    Writer-editor Vivian Warby, another poet, says: "The more I try to silence the words, the louder they become until I write them down. "Only then do they become quiet."

CHAPTER 12

EARTH QUEEN

"The Earth is a loving mother, nurturing and protecting all peoples and species without discrimination. When you realize the Earth is so much more than simply your environment, you'll protect her in the same way as you would yourself."
– THICH NHAT HANH

Some European restaurants specialize in sightless dining. Smell, taste, and touch inform your perceptions, stimulating a renewed appreciation of life in color with the lifting of the blindfold.

Such experiential treats come free in Johannesburg, thanks to ubiquitous blackouts. Minus, of course, the solicitous service and tasty morsels. Just shin and toe guidance to negotiate the dark where feline regurgitations of the rodent variety lurk.

These are not the sole connections you want.

We all have our paths to tread. Learning to observe my world through the spectacles of self-love expanded my vision in a way no optometrist could. None so blind as those who choose not to see, but that's okay. We all go at our own pace.

In the murk of winter, I traverse an expanse of the veld near the stream or Spruit in the Delta Park to meet my walking amigas, Uscha and Phillippa.

Only the occasional rattle of urban surfers dragging their recycling trolleys along rutted paths punctuates the pre-dawn quiet. Alone with my thoughts, each step into the dark feels like the writing process.

Fear rustles in the long grass, chills my neck with cold fingers.

I am not my angst. Inhale. Exhale. Level up. Shift fear to curiosity. Contemplate cave-sized vaginas – the Nenkovo Rock Womb in Bulgaria and gigantic stone creatures like Heimaey elephant-shaped rock in Iceland.

Africa, too, is shaped like an elephant's head. It's all perspective. I know so little of our ancient past, yet it tugs at my mind like a restless bedmate.

It's not what any history book taught me, that's for sure. Sally Jane Delaney, also known as BioGeology Girl, offers compelling evidence on her Facebook group #Biogeology that rocks, mountains, and even continents were once live people and animals.

The size of these beings is almost beyond comprehension. Islands of knowledge emerge from tumultuous seas, sustaining me with the swaying palm perspective of a pina colada cocktail served in a coconut.

The Earth is my mother; I shall not want. She makes me in physical form. In rich soil, She roots me; Her quiet waters soothe me. Her body nourishes mine.

Nature defies deaf Phoenicians. Both formless and form, Earth speaks in rushing rivers, crackling fires, and crowing cocks at dawn.

I'm learning to listen and incorporate it all. My connection to Mother Earth guides my every step.

The Delta has always been magical to me. Once, when we were newly married and broke, my husband found US6000 discarded in the long grass. He used the money to buy a plane ticket to Copenhagen, where he found work, a turning point in our fortunes.

On another dawn walk, Uscha and I watched a brown hyena – one of the world's rarest creatures, drinking from the stream. She, too, found temporary solace here.

City cameras captured her wandering the streets, even crossing the Magistrate's Court steps before Johannesburg Zoo staff took her away in a van. I think about her often.

In late Summer, I weave through swathes of pink and white Spring Cosmos flowers and crunch over the brittle frost of Autumn veld. Irrespective of the season – 'see sun' – I walk barefoot to watch the sunrise.

The Sun is my social media – my *raison d'etre* – speaking in frequency, affirming my sovereignty, dispersing shadows in its golden energy.

My soles draw in Earth's magnetic resonance as sparkling sunbeams line-dance on the dam. Diamonds ripple. Rising vapor bathes the landscape in a warm glow. The fire in my belly ignites – the waters of my being flow. I feel alive, my frequencies super-charged; all systems go!

There was much to undo when I removed my blindfold of beliefs to let Gaia excise the cataracts of characters blocking my vision.

Still seeking resolution or retribution, long-held identities with their unhealthy fixations and dependencies fell through the trapdoor of my expanding reality with shrieks, wails, and gnashing of teeth. All gone! What took me so long?

Do I miss them? Dear me, no. Like a fading blister, I registered their departure with relief.

Those who remained in my life no longer depended on me needing them, which ironically made for healthier relationships.

Now, my only real relationship is with me. If human history is a "Gaian dream," I unfurled with the leaves.[1]

I have begun to identify as a tree – solitary and alienated on the surface but deeply interconnected with sister forests across the Earth. Our far-reaching roots share the sap of our Source connections rising through spinal trunks, branching out in boughs, receiving and transmitting Love.

We nourish one another through the changing seasons. Fanciful? Me? The echoing crags of my mother-tree laughter rebound.

Pre-Christian Pagans appealed to arboreal spirits for favors or protection long before the Abrahamic religions told us who to worship. I am the tree, and the tree is me.

---

1   McKenna, n.d.

Merging into Mother Earth's larger bandwidth surges my creative power and helps me hold my ground in these times of upheaval.

We mother trees – walking, standing – will win in the end. Count on it. Being grounded sets me free to fly. I am pregnant with ideas – a fecundity of creative paths opens new routes to serendipity.

What else could there possibly be but Nature and me? I command the wind; exhale hurricanes, blow hot and cold. The cooling lava from my volcanic rages replenishes the soil of my being in rivers.

As things once held dear become air, my great mother's sap of purity evolves, transforms, and nourishes me.

She incinerates everything incomplete. She re-leafs me in her embrace of new possibilities and ideas. We were here before the infiltration and deceit. I bow to no external authority demanding improvement when there's nothing wrong with me.

Oh, the arrogance, the ignominy, the conceit!

My connection with Nature was always there. But I was battling too many loosh-harvesting identities to be aware.

Now that I know that predatory timeline with its ever-tightening restrictions, slavish identities, and trembling dependencies is not mine, I pay it no mind.

I identify my place within each element – the note in the symphony, the spark in the flame, constantly partaking of Mother Earth's life-sustaining resources.

I am not in my body. My body is in Me!

I don't recall when I made the shift and stepped barefoot into this gorgeous new frequency, but I'm here now. Now here. Know where.

And everything's all right. By sharing the hygge, I embody the light. My source connection nourishes my heart.

There's more than enough hygge to go around. The thing about learning new stuff is that you knew it already on some level.

We are seasonal beings, connected with Mother Earth through our relationships with her elements. My best memories are grounded in forest, snow, and desert.

How did I get here? I took the fast train through the doom merchant territories without stopping at any news corporation station.

Confronted by the citizens of Naysayer, I stood my ground, and the effect was two-fold. Most removed their frequency from my biofield. Their departures only further strengthened my resolve not to self-censor.

What did I lose in the process? Oh, I don't know – remnants of trauma-addicted slave-self identities, all the Not Me's and their anxieties. I lost the need to please. Yeah, good riddance to that one.

What did I find? Sovereign surfers riding transmutational waves alongside me, a more expanded sense of myself within a glowing bandwidth of continuity.

It's as though an electrician went into my ceiling and rewired everything to better connect with my multi-dimensional self. And my thinking went from fuzzy to clear.

Earth

EMBRACE *your sovereignty. Eschew practices or products denigrating Mother Earth's resources. Support sovereign beings in the currencies of their choice instead of corporate enslavement.*

ALIGN *yourself with like-minded people who share your vision for living in Nature's World Order.*

RECALIBRATE. *Recognize harmful habits. Make kinaesthetic changes to bring yourself into balance and realize your power.*

TRANSMUTE *Trust and accept whatever Nature sweeps from your life. Loss can be painful, but it's how new growth and expansion patterns begin.*

HARVEST *food from the wild or your garden, process your plants and flowers for remedies. Honor your intuition. The more you do, the louder it will speak to you*

Earth Queen

"Her feet touch the Earth. The wind fills her lungs. Mother Earth's precious life-sustaining resources bring form and structure to her dreams."

Quiver arrows:
Generosity, practicality, superhuman strength, the ability to turn thoughts into forms.

Archetype:
Gaia, Earth Mother of creation

REFERENCES

Chapter 10 Earth Awareness

Basu, C. (2017, January 30). Loss of trees driving giraffes to a toxic diet. Retrieved from biosphere online: http://www.biosphereonline.com/2017/01/30/giraffes-are-vulnerable-to-change/

Gagliano, M. (2022). Monica Gagliano. Retrieved from monicagagliano.com/

Jacqueline, oraclegirl.org. Retrieved from Oracle Girl: https://www.oraclegirl.org/library

Jstor. (n.d.). Acacia trees kill antelope. Retrieved from Jstor.org:

KAY, J. (n.d.). Quantum Truths JC Kay. Retrieved from Youtube: https://m.youtube.com/channel/UCSgG-_Eqf9cfBBZg_4104WQ

Kinzler, D. (2018, November 10). Are trees communicating? Research says yes. Retrieved from Allen Larocque. Retrieved from Allen Larocque: http://www.allenlarocque.ca/

Ryan, V. G. (2021). The Mind of Plants: Narratives of Vegal Intelligence. Synergetic Press. Shanon, B. (2016, March 20).

The Bible's Moses Was On DMT Says Hebrew Professor. Retrieved from A New Understanding: https://www.anewunderstanding.org/single-post/2016/05/28/

Simard, S. (2021). Finding the Mother Tree: Discovering the Wisdom of the Forest. Knopf.

The Mother Tree project. (n.d.). Retrieved from mothertreeproject.org/

Wikipedia. (n.d.). Arbor vitae (anatomy). wikipedia.org/wiki/Arbor_vitae_(anatomy)

YouTube. (2021, October 28). The mind of plants book launch. Retrieved from YouTube:

Chapter 11 Solid Grounding

American Chiropractic Association. (2022). Back Pain Facts and Statistics. Retrieved from Hands Down Better:

acatoday.org/Patients/What-is-Chiropractic/Back-Pain-Facts-and-Statistics

Carey, S. (n.d.).Alexander Technique in Everyday Activity. Retrieved from Hite: https://hiteltd.co.uk/webshop/books/

Complete Guide to the Alexander Technique. (n.d.). Alexander Technique.

Retrieved from Alexander Technique dot com: https://www.alexandertechnique.com/at/ D.P.M, W. A. (n.d.).

Why shoes make normal gait impossible. Retrieved from correcttoes.com:
 https://www.correcttoes.com/foot-help/wp-content/uploads/2015/12/rossiWhyShoesMakeNormal-GaitImpossible.pdf

Jacqueline, oraclegirl.org. J. (2021, July 19). Your Self Healing Abilities with Dr. Northrup. Retrieved from Oracle Girl: https://www.oraclegirl.org/library/your-self-healing-ability

Li, Q. (2009, March 25). Effect of forest bathing trips on human immune function. Retrieved from US National Library of Medicine: https://www.ncbi.nlm.nih.gov/pmc/articles/PMC2793341/

Louv, R. (2016). Last Child in the Woods. Retrieved from Richard Louv: http://richardlouv.com

Northrup, D. C. (2021, July 19). Your Self Healing Ability. Retrieved from Oracle Girl: https://www.oraclegirl.org/library/your-self-healing-ability

Ober, C. (2010). Earthing The most important health discovery ever. Laguna Beach: Basic Health Publications.

Rasmussen, C. A. (2019, October 11). Association of Neurocognitive and Physical Function With Gait Speed in Midlife.

Retrieved from Jama Network Open: https://jamanetwork.com/journals/jamanetworkopen/fullarticle/2752818?resultClick=3

Ruth, G. (n.d.). Attention Restoration Theory: A systematic review.

Retrieved from ecehh.org: https://www.ecehh.org/research/
attention-restoration-theory-a-systematic-review/
Simard, S. (2021). Secrets of a Tree Whisperer. Retrieved from Nexus Newsfeed: https://nexusnews-
feed.com/
Warrior29. (2021, April 27). Twitter.com/Warrior2913/status/1386821191479046150?s=20

Chapter 12 Earth Queen

Hanh, T. N. (2015). Falling In Love With The Earth by Thich Nhat Hanh. Retrieved from Written for
Paris Climate Talk in 2015: https://thichnhathanhquotecollective.com/
McKenna, T. (n.d.). Terence McKenna Quotes. Retrieved from Goodreads:

SECTION V

METAL

The electromagnetic properties of Metal fuse the Chinese fifth element with the Hindu concept of Akasha, meaning aether or permeability.

Also known as Plasma, it combines the first four elements and the love consciousness of the sixth.

Aether, composed of hydrogen, is another form of Water. Both elements share healing, regenerative properties, hold consciousness, and memory

CHAPTER 13

THE GOLD STANDARD

"The Sword in the Stone is the iron in your hemoglobin. The Lady of the Lake is your heart. Your will is forged in the heart, and you pull Excalibur from the stone to rule your body."
— JAMES TRUE

You're full of metal. Countries harvest titanium, copper, gold, and palladium from human ashes in crematoriums to melt in foundries and re-use in the construction of road signs and electric cars. Talk about upcycling your hip replacement![1]

The muscular and nervous systems work with the electrical potential to animate our bodies. We are voltages, producing electricity through the interaction of aether and metals in our blood (plasma) working with nerve impulses.

The gold in every human brain and heart cavity receives and transmits love via electrical signals.

---

1 McCracken, 2018

Our electromagnetic biofield – aura – from Au (meaning gold, hence the chemistry symbol) and Ra, the sun god – also sounds like ore, another gold metaphor.

So, we power the universe, for better or worse.

Consciously switching on your connection with the gold frequency accelerates your ability to self-heal, activates your instructions, and deletes redundant identities.

"(When) you realize you only lose what was never you, you can re-engineer your Source connection's wiring to change your physical body to accommodate the increased frequency of your multi-dimensional Self," says Jacqueline.

"You become a self-generating unit interwoven with the gold frequency."

This alchemical process increases the ability of all beings in relationship with the elements to generate more physical gold on earth.[2]

Gold is malleable and reflective. We, too, reflect – like phase conjugate mirrors – everything in our world from different angles or points of view.

Mirrors represent a vortex into parallel worlds. That's why magicians used them to scry. In *Through the Looking Glass*, Alice moves through a mirror into an alternative reality.

Double-sided mirrors can magnify a haunt of energetic impressions in the reflected world.

You, sovereign queen, must determine their source to fend off any attack.

Lewis Carroll describes the world – "if this is the world at all, you know" – as a chess game.[3]

Looking into a mirror to see behind you is a traditional way to spy. You need a rearview to drive.

Sunlight glinting on a mirror can start a fire faster than quicksilver.

---

2   Jacqueline, oraclegirl.org Track of the month 4, 2021
3   Lewis, n.d.

Mercury Rising

Once an essential component of mirrors, mercury, called Makaradhwaja in India, is prized as "the best alchemical drug of longevity," despite its much-vaunted toxicity.

Makaradhwaja began eternal life alchemy, synthesizing red colloidal gold with gold to render body and soul everlasting, according to S Mahdihassan.[4]

Makara was an Indian god of fertility. His Greek, Roman, Nordic, and Germanic counterparts are Hermes, Mercury, Oden, and Woden. Wednesday – Mercredi – is named after them.

Hermes (god of roads) is etymologically related to the Russian surname Putin (Путин), meaning путь "way, path, the road."[5]

President Vladimir Putin is famous for saying: "Nobody and nothing will stop Russia on the road to strengthening democracy."[6]

Etymologically Mercury from the Latin Mercurius relates to merchandise and border. Conveyor of thieves and messengers to the underworld, Mercury the merchant, "keeper of boundaries," bridged two realms and controlled the flow of information.[7]

Is that why so many newspapers have Mercury in their titles?

Born Maria Salomea Sklodowska, Marie Curie, the Polish-born French physicist famous for her research into radioactivity, polonium, and radium, twice won the Nobel Prize.

Read Marie Curie's famous quote out loud. "Be less curious about people and more curious about ideas."

More curious – *mer curius*. Marie Curie – Mar Curie – *Mer Cury*. Is that just a phonetic coincidence? I don't think so.

You can literally "s-e-a" the sound of 'mer' right there.

Born Farrokh Bulsara, the rock star Freddie Mercury allegedly chose the appellation Mercury, for himself.

---

4   S, 1985
5   wiktionary, n.d.
6   Brainy Quote, n.d.
7   Mythopedia, n.d.

Queen's lead guitarist Brian May said his *My Fairy King* song inspired the name change, while astrologists claimed it was because Mercury ruled the Sun in Freddie's birth chart.[8]

I met Freddie Mercury in 1984 at a small press conference when Queen performed in Sun City.

His conversational strut was cockerel confident as he deflected a barrage of questions with sizzling velocity.

"Have I ever hit a woman? Not when she was down, dears."

"Do I intend to father children? Well, no. Not when you can buy them from Harrods."

Even as he wiped his armpits on the late Sol Kerzner's crisp white linen tablecloth, his magnetizing energy and dazzling vitality mesmerized us all.

I described him in *The Star* newspaper as "like quicksilver, impossible to suppress."

He was, without doubt, a magnificent showman, but was he also a brilliant actor?

Using an overlay of teeth, researcher Mark Tokarski lays out a compelling case for Freddie Mercury being a twin, faking his death in 1991, and reinventing himself as TV psychologist Dr. Phil, introduced to the world by Oprah Winfrey Show in the late 1990s.[9]

Is this the reel life? See the opening lines of *Bohemian Rhapsody*.

Do lifetime actors play archetypes on a world stage? Could Mercury and other elements be pantheons?

Thorium derives its name from the Norse god Thor, Iridium from the Greek goddess Iris. Helium relates to the sun deity Helios. Other examples abound.

Mercury is non-reflective, attracts gold, and increases radio wave reception. Mercury ore derived from cinnabar, a transformation stone, is essential in generating free energy.

The Benben stone helped create Earth, according to Heliopolitan and Eygptian myth. Kept in the temple of Heliopolis, home to the sun god

---

8   Iscan, 2021
9   Tokarski, 2016

Ra (also Re) near the Nile Delta, the Benben bestowed magical powers and enlightenment to anybody in its vicinity.

Today, Benben's whereabouts are a mystery. Wim Godgevlamste speculates the black cube of Mecca contains a few small bits, while the rest of it could be in London, under the throne in the House of Lords. Is it kept close for coronation ceremonies? Who knows?[10]

The three-meter-high gilded Helios statue standing on a ball-earth in the BBC (British Broadcasting Centre) rotunda represents "the radiation of television light around the world."

Helios is the fountain's focal point.

"Two reclining figures beneath the fountain bowl represent sound and vision, the two components of television." [11]

What if broadcasting were an amplified version of spell casting – hooking and harvesting the prana – "plasmic belief goo" – of our attention under the guise of news and entertainment?

Radio Goo Goo. Radio Ga Ga. Black Goo. Grey Goo. Lady Gaga. Google. Yuri Gagarin, the Russian astronaut who died in 1968 and uncannily resembled Neil Armstrong. And – *quelle surprise* – Gagarin's listed on the IMDb too.

So much sentimental goo-ga!

Not the guru but the true goo

Ah, but what of true goo, not the guru but life's plasmic goo that connects us to everything?

A consommé of positively charged particles (ions) and negatively charged particles (electrons), Plasma glows in the stars, nebulas, auroras, lightning, the sun, and the moon.[12]

The same plasma in our blood comprising our visible universe holds our memories.

---

10   godgevlamste, 2022
11   Cooper, 2017
12   News-in-depth, 2019

No wonder the electricity of our attention is catnip to corporates. They bank on your compliance because they need you to manifest reality for them. You're the dream machine, remember.

Our life force, aka gold frequency, imbues whatever we focus on with pure plasmic power and atomic intelligence.

That's why a homemade gift or jewelry from a beloved partner, friend, or family member, holds more prana than a shop-bought afterthought.

As individual notes within nature's symphony, we create prana as we broadcast sound and light through the filters of our perceptions.

We tune in, process, and project the interpretation of our beliefs into manifestation.

Creation is an eternal spiral of aether moving into the fire, air, water, and earth that filters through your antenna's unique metal frames of reference, including gold in your brain and heart cavities.[13]

Author Leanne Babcock relies on the gold of her inner guidance when working with shamanic tools and brain science.

"What lies beneath your thoughts and emotions is consciousness – your true self.

"When you slow down to connect with this consciousness, beyond the busyness of the mind, you access this deep inner wisdom," she says. "This inner wisdom, your intuition, offers a far more expanded reality than the linear flow of information received and processed by the logical mind.

"Your brain processes concepts and stories from the realm of information you're ingesting. Your consciousness taps into and assimilates those frequencies, which your body integrates.

"Intuition offers a far more expanded reality than the linear flow of information. We have to offload the fears and blockages that leaden our energy.

"The more you become a closer vibrational match with your Divine Natural Self, the more your consciousness shifts you into a calmer, blissful state.

---

13   Jacqueline, oraclegirl.org 2021

"Awareness of your relationship with the elements transforms your timeline from mundane to magical."[14]

Animals sense the magnetic forces and fields through which the Earth operates. So could we, if we could find our center again.

How to Create Prana at Home:

Prana is a natural self-creating process, so you don't have to do anything, but if you'd like to generate more of the good stuff around your environment, here are a few tips.

1. *Springcleaning creates prana because you purify yourself and your surroundings. Decluttering does the same.*

2. *Put thought into all your interactions with people that love you. Whatever you nurture, write, post, or share, you create and imbue with the prana of your belief.*

3. *You change the pranic energy when you own your actions or give yourself credit.*

4. *Silver, gold, and copper transmit or hold prana for longer. Gold treats anxiety, while fiery metals like copper and zinc create a healing electromagnetic charge.*

5. *Storing things in copper or silver utensils kills bacteria. Wearing a copper bangle can help with arthritis, inflammation, and skin ailments.*

6. *The more you tune into the Golden Frequency that connects all nature's beings, the more golden prana you generate.*

---

14   Babcock, 2017

METAL WORK

The Inner Cannon, or five-element personality system, is a 2000-year-old medical text by Chinese physicians and scholars theorizing that Water, Wood, Fire, Earth, and Metal compose the universal forces.

Dondi Dahlin, a historic preservationist, performer, author, and daughter of Donna Eden, founder of Eden Energy Medicine, travels the world presenting international workshops with her mother.[15]

She says she grew up knowing about the five elements but only began to apply them to her life in her early 20s on a road trip with her family and an irritating boyfriend. Dondi realized he had all the trappings of "an imbalanced water element."

By combining each element and its associated personality type to create an individual psychology profile, Dondi realized she had a system to understand men for life and found compassion for all people. "My five-element system enabled me to perceive things so that I no longer needed to vilify anyone for their behavior. I could tell which element – water, fire, wood, earth, or metal predominated in their personalities.

Superpowers can become super challenges when one element is out of whack in human personalities," she says. "All five components are within you. Under stress, people will default to one element.

Water withdraws, wood gets angry, fire may panic or scatter, earth smothers or nags, and metal personalities detach.

"Confusion over the action and behaviors of others is what polarizes us," says Dondi, who teaches others how to test which elements predominate in every individual. Her mission is to help others awaken from the illusion of separation.

"The five elements offer superpowers and super challenges. Understanding both will add another arrow to your quill."

Here is her list of the superpowers and challenges of each predominant element[16].

---

15   Dahlin, Five Day Elements, n.d.
16   Dahlin, 2016

ELEMENTAL FACETS

Water:
SUPER POWERS: *Deep thinking, intuitive, creative, philosophical*
CHALLENGE: *Fear.*
HANDLING TIP: *"Give them time undisturbed.*
Fear of change or abandonment causes procrastination and indecision.
Water personalities need to withdraw and come back to themselves.
Let them know you are there and remind them they are not alone."

Wood:
SUPER POWERS: *Hard working, uber-organized.*
CHALLENGE: *Quick to anger*
HANDLING TIP: *Be upbeat. Give frequent acknowledgments.*
Pats on the back and high-fives go a long way.

Fire:
SUPER POWERS: *Optimism, lightness, and warmth*
CHALLENGE: *Easily scattered and distracted. Quick to panic.*
HANDLING TIP: *Be precise with fire personalities. Don't coddle.*
Fire personalities have a hard time going to the negatives – lace in
laughter, love, and lightness to keep them present.

Earth:
SUPER POWERS: *nurturance, generosity, compassion*
CHALLENGES: *Over worry. Too much reliance on the past.*
Enable undesirable behavior because of their need to be loved.
HANDLING TIP: *Challenge them on their co-dependent cycles.*

Metal:
SUPER POWERS: *Wisdom, grace under pressure, calm, meticulous*
CHALLENGES: *Aoofness, detachment.*
HANDLING TIP: *Give them space, and see their grace as a gift.*

Four Metal Affirmations:

1. *I am a connoisseur of the finest metals.*
2. *I trust my internal guidance system*
3. *I see life from all sides*
4. *I am flexible and strong.*

CHAPTER 14

METAL QUEEN

*"Love gives birth to water, fire, air, earth, and metal.
They dance within you, bringing the sixth element of
Mother Earth consciousness."*
— ORACLE GIRL

Metal Queen sounds more like a bedframe than a royal identity. I wouldn't relinquish my sovereignty for a plane ticket, so I'm hardly going to swap it for some Sealy Posturepedic dream.

Besides, isn't it pointless now to identify as an individual Queen? We're unique composites of all six elements.

Paradoxically, that's the point. Or node of you, if you prefer. See the double-sun in 'prefer' and how node anagrams into done. Forgive me; it's just the way I read nowadays.

Done implies completion, but like perfection, it's a static concept, making language an inadequate tool to unearth nature's deep mysteries. Do you need to understand?

I don't think so. After all, you don't need to know how electricity works to switch on a light.

Being connected to nature's pure love frequency brings me everything I require – when I need it. The trick is to relax. We tune in like antennae to nature's golden frequency.

Layered into our blood, our DNA's electrically-charged particles – the antenna or live wire part of us – connect with and filter nature's universal mainframe through shifting perspectives.

So we are both motionless and mobile, wave and particle.[1]

"The waters in your blood carry the gold frequency that turns your body into a live antenna broadcasting to all beings," says Jacqueline. "We flow with the constant undoing, transmutation, and generation of nature's cycles fixed – as we are – on the Existence Grid."[2]

Origins or oro-djinns?

Nature's progeny dies in time yet lives in timelessness. We alter and dissipate life's dream fragments in the wake of an expanding current of continuity.

Thus we are both alive and dead, mortal and immortal, visible and invisible. We are single and multiple, everything and nothing. Indefinable.

At least, that's my innerstanding when I ponder my origins or oro-djinns. The way it's pronounced hints at gold (oro) spirits (djinn). I sense plunder of the gold rather than reciprocity.

Are we the gold? Am I just being fanciful?

The more I tune into my gold frequency, the more information I need comes from inside me.

I am also a pure note in the universe, not just a node.

My biological mother labored to birth my physical body, but that was not the beginning of me. Any 'beginnings' outside nature's infinite gold frequency bandwidth can only be temporary.

The emergence of my vessel through a portal of opposites into this spacetime frame is not my totality. How can it be?

---

1   Richardson, 2014
2   Jacqueline, oraclegirl.org2021

Chained between divisive concepts, I became enslaved until I began to take my power back. There's no need for hierarchy or external authority along the journey of self-discovery.

There is no me in vibRAtion, only Ra. I identify as river, tree, fire, and frequency.

All elements contain the Ra or Re. All, including me, are intertwined with the Sun's golden energy.

There was a time I confused fool's gold for the real thing – Love for Haddaway theme song variations – until I realized my connection with Source was all the Love I'd ever need.

That strength determined all the scenery in my emotional theatre. My relationships became healthier when I dissolved my dependence on others to experience a better life.

Their automatic responses convinced me some were more human than others, so there was nothing to take personally.

New embodied consciousness appeared in their wake, often in the same people. When sunlight seeps through the forest foliage surrounding your temples (on either side of your head), your bonds with Nature's Pure Love frequency strengthen.

Your unique path becomes clear, both on inner and outer levels. Your relationship with the elements increases your ability to experience, receive, and transmit Love – Hygge – as I like to call it.

As I level up, the world levels up to meet me. The Sun and its corona annihilate the slave-setting, deleting the dross in a shimmering golden sea of frequency.

Out with the grime. In with the shine.

Love embodies, purifies, and switches on my ability to heal. My strength increases within the silent truth of who and what I am – an antenna tuned to nature's infinite frequency – a flame within a spark, an ocean within a drop, a continuous purification that never begun and can never end.

METAL

MASTER *the narrative stream. We are magnetic beings. Merging with all the elements increases my gold frequency.*

EXPRESS *nature's love that's been with you from the beginning and brought you here.*

TUNE **IN** *to nature's transformative truth and trust the process.*

ANCHOR *the force of nature at the higher levels and bring it into being.*

LET *go of old habits and ways of being. If you don't, you will lose the bond of affection with yourself.*

THE METAL QUEEN

'Awake to her power, she forges inclusive new ways of being.'

Quiver arrows:
Strength, malleability, reflectiveness, resonance, magnetism, fluidity.

Archetype:
The Metal Queen encompasses all the aforementioned elemental archetypes from a plasmic perspective.

REFERENCES

Chapter 13 The Gold Standard

@jarue369. (2022, February 22). Quote retrieved from Twitter: https://twitter.com/jarue3

Babcock, L. (2017). Open Me, a daring and magical journey from fear to freedom. Leanne Babcock.

Brainy Quote. (n.d.). Vladimir Putin Quotes. Retrieved from Brainy quotes.

Cooper, G. (2017). A famous sculpture returns to the BBC Television Centre. My London News.

Dahlin, D. (2016). The Five Elements. TarcherPerigee. Dahlin, D. (n.d.).

Five Day Elements. Retrieved from YouTube: https://www.youtube.com/channel/UCJyC4m1nyCgGQl9xGtmvxLQ/featured

godgevlamste. (2022, January). Crater Earth: in search of the BenBen stone (final part). Retrieved from YouTube: https://www.youtube.com/watch?v=8HTS_essPao

Jacqueline, oraclegirl.org (2021). Track of the month 4. Retrieved from Oracle Girl: oraclegirl.org/library/

Jacqueline, oraclegirl.org (2021, December 13). Track of the Month 4. Retrieved from oraclegirl.org/library/

Iscan, M. (2021). The Reason Why Freddie Mercury Changed His Birth Name 'Farrokh Bulsara.' Rock Celebrities.

Tokarski, M. (2016). Freddie Mercury became Dr. Phil McGraw: Case Closed. Piece of Mindful. https://pieceofmindful.com/tag/farrokh-bulsara/

Lewis, C. (n.d.). Through the Looking-Glass. Retrieved from Spark Notes:

McCracken, N. (2018). The metal finding new life after cremation. BBC News.

Mythopedia. (n.d.). Mercury Roman God. Retrieved from Mythopedia: https://mythopedia.com/topics/mercury

News-In-depth, A. (2019, March 28).1965 scientist claims the moon is plasma, landing on it won't be possible | RetroFocus. Retrieved from YouTube: https://www.youtube.com/watch?v=1oCNGcbwxW-g&t=54s S, M. (1985).

National Library of Medicine. Retrieved from pubmed.ncbi.nlm:

https://pubmed.ncbi.nlm.nih.gov/?term=Mahdihassan+S&cauthor_id=3895885

wiktionary. (n.d.). Путин. Retrieved from wiktionary.

Chapter 14 Metal Queen

Jacqueline, oraclegirl.org (2021, December 13). Track of the month 4..Oraclegirl.org/library/track-of-the-month-4

Richardson, J. (2014, November 27). We are frequency vibration, and DNA is the antenna. Retrieved from Natural Life Energy: https://www.naturallifeenergy.com/frequency-vibration-dna-antenna/

SECTION VI

HYGGE

Hygge, or ultimate nourishment, encompasses the entire quantum field of pure love, moving plasmic aetheric space into the fire, air, water, earth, and precious metal elements in an evolving cycle.

CHAPTER 15

HIGHWAY TO HYGGE

"The human body resonates at the same frequency as Mother Earth. (She) will exist with or without us. Yet if she is sick, it is because mankind is sick and separated. And if our vibrations are bad, she reacts to it, as do all living creatures."
– SUZY KASSEM, RISE UP AND SALUTE THE SUN

Change is possible only if you recognize you are not separate from Earth's elements, animals, and people. Your strength and awakening come about when you merge all notions of being and non-being, creator and creature, mind, spirit, me, and you.

Just as the fifth element is interchangeable with metal or aether, the sixth element, a plasmic ether of pure Love and Possibility encompassing the entire quantum field, can be seen as Mother Earth Consciousness, Nature, or Hygge.

The first four elements relate to life and growing things on Earth – "the brute bulk of our world" containing precious metals, gold, ores, and crystals within its geology.

Metal, aether, or plasma are interchangeable. The sixth element constantly cycles space into the fire, air, water, earth, and metal elements. In the silence between the notes is where you meet everyone you ever lost.

You "innnerstand" you encompass them all within you and experience your relationship with them more intimately than before or the last time you encountered them.

They re-appear in new forms, different guises, and you recognize them through their essence as your golden frequency bridges duality. All moments merge into one continuous purifying stream.

CLARITY AND CONNECTION

Clarity is seeing – without looking back – your history washed clean. You embody more love in the sparkling wake of Mother Earth's ever-expanding consciousness.

She's fierce. She doesn't fuck around. Like you, She's upgrading too, transmuting her physical form to hold the new frequencies of nature's order flooding in.

Visit a few stops if you like – Chi Gong, Reiki, Judo, whatever floats your boat – but don't stay too long in any one place because, says Jacqueline, you become the image of whatever you take on. "If you concretize and cement yourself to just that image, you form another slave self."

Always trust what your body says when co-opting with others.

Don't go there if the pure love element is absent as you relate to it. And never take anything onboard unless it aligns with who you already are. Your gut never lies to you.

A queen needs no system. You are becoming your unique version of pure love itself. The old world is the circus leaving town. And good riddance to colonist rubbish!

Now that you're starting to see, you realize you're becoming more than you ever dreamed you could be. And it's as though you're only just begun.

Consciousness is a blend of purity and impurity, neither pristine perfection nor ultimate state.

The Greek philosopher Empedocles – inventor of rhetoric and founder of medical science in Italy – said Earth, Air, Fire, and Water form everything around us.

"Love brings it together. Strife keeps it apart."[1]

The six elements communicate with you from the inside out.

Jacqueline explains that your infinity spark powers up materiality as the sun and waters of your being interact with your receptive, creative aspect.

"It happens every day as the sun (the light of you) in congress with water (your blood) moves your infinity spark into material existence via the gold frequency.

"Nodes form and individuate in the global nature intelligence system."

While pure love allows new things to come into form, it will not happen for you if you're not open to this possibility.

I find the more I connect my bare soles with the Earth, grounding Her love into my being, the more beams of a golden frequency seem to dance around me, glinting like sunlight through the leaves. As Jacqueline puts it: "It's about how you root in this Earth and the continued generation and conscious manifestation of your life aligned with everything that honors Nature's principles."[2]

Operating from a *hyggelig* space oversees the best way forward for you and everyone else in your world as you discover the interconnectedness in your sovereignty.

"Pure love and possibility is the sixth element that introduces you to the whole of the quantum field, which has merged for the first time with Mother Earth Consciousness.

"Space and aether carry that substance of Mother Earth consciousness (which) powers down into the density of material form (to generate) new future timelines.

Nature is neither a religion nor a spiritual pathway, so there is nothing to work out, nothing to activate or ponder for years. Purification happens whether you're ready or not.

---

1   encyclopedia, n.d.
2   Jacqueline, oraclegirl.org 2021

Anything not aligned with Nature's World Order will come under more pressure and have less room for maneuver in the outside world. "There's no pathway to your Self; there is only you being you," says Jacqueline.[3]

"Love gives birth to water, fire, air to earth, and metal. They dance within you, bringing the sixth element of Mother Earth's consciousness. Every time you cross paths with a frequency that sees you embody more love, you generate the sixth element through the act of making something real in this world."

Six natural hygge principles

1. *Nourishes and sustains you, being your only trustworthy source of love.*
2. *Tempers conflict, struggle, and contradiction*
3. *Transmutes any situation*
4. *Becomes fiercer, more powerful, harsh, and uncompromising.*
5. *Upgrades and transmute physical form to handle new higher frequencies.*
6. *It gives you what you need.*

Four Hygge Affirmations:

1. *My connection with Source nourishes and sustains me, providing everything I need.*
2. *I can transmute conflict, struggle, and contradiction in any situation.*
3. *I am becoming fiercer and more powerful every day.*
4. *My physical form is constantly upgrading to handle new higher frequencies.*

---

3   Jacqueline, oraclegirl.org. 2021

CHAPTER 16

HYGGE QUEEN

"Pervasive silence. Rich contentment.
Everything given, and everything taken away."
– ORACLE GIRL

The Hygge Queen encompasses the first four elemental sovereigns in ever-changing combinations. The fifth and sixth elements purify her, constantly reshaping the patterns of her reality via her Source connection.

She is spark and flame, raindrop and cloud, a single note in a symphony of sound. She is subject only to nature. She walks barefoot on the ground.

Meet the new me, nothing like the old me struggling with authority. Now that I identify with Mother Earth Consciousness in action and repose, my power asserts itself in non-compliance at every turn.

She is both inside and outside of me. I generate the cosmic intelligence of myself and nature in multi-dimensional frequency. Cool or what?

215

Blows kiss at the conjugate mirror reflecting myriad me's Pretentious? *Mais, absolutement, mes cheries!*

That spark of infinity holding my life instructions determines my relationship with everything, including the sun, moon, and stars.

Everything is in a relationship with me. How did I get here?

By default, I guess. There were no big fireworks – bar sustaining self-revelatory moments. When the road forked, I took the No Way bus to a Sovereign city the controllers tried to bury in cultural quicksand.

I met friendly and not-so-friendly frequencies at the confluence of the individual and collective rivers.

New embodied consciousness stepping off the boat led to something unexpected. All shared time with me and connected with how I function. I merged with some energies to embody more love. Others I released to the fast-flowing currents accordingly.

I've seen how the colonist parasite hides in sentimentality. Once I realized I'd been doing things this way all along, I stepped onto the platform for the next stage of my expanded life.

The recognition that others were just another version of me made it easy. And while my way is best for me, it's not the only way. You have your way.

We each forge our pathways according to our relationship with nature's principles, individual instructions, and where we connect with the gold frequency highway to hygge.

Like decluttering stuff no longer fit for purpose, nature's purifying perfection first undoes then upgrades you. I reveled in the space that appeared when I stopped struggling and let nature's take-no-prisoner frequencies transmute me.

We guardians and scribes write what we like.

The old Draconian world order is a passing show, a circus on its way out of town.

The only governing bodies I respect are the waters of Earth. To hell with it. We will take things from here.

Mine is not the only way, and neither is yours. There is no pathway. There's only ever been me being me. Or you being you – no history – only your story and mine.

Who needs history when you can enter and leave one reality from so many points of view?

When you surf an event's frequency waves without forgetting yourself in the slam dunk splutter, the fiery heat of your inner sun renders any experience invalid.

It's a re-versed future rewrite. How I craved that gift before I realized it was mine all along. We've always been able to sing another song or write another stanza. Hooray!

No wonder our history, culture, and education came prescribed. The controllers didn't want us aligning with our true divinity.

Dear me, no. That would render their take-over attempts of our environment insignificant. Well, tough titty!

I could not co-parent with corporate governments hellbent on tyranny, so I withdrew all consent. A whisper at first, then a shout, but the more I said no, the more others spoke out. The old world cracked like an eggshell.

Normal became extraordinary as reality bent to my decree and hygge found me. What a win! My relationship with nature is all there ever is, was, and will be. Nothing – least of all my perception of myself – is fixed. I can prove my existence from cradle to my current age, yet I am alive and dead. That's the paradox.

I traversed the dry, shifting sands of my senses, searched for myself in sunlight and shadows, and died 1000 times, but it was no big deal.

I'm here now – now here –in all my glorious imperfection. Forged by fire, strengthened by steel, clarity, and connection.

The miraculous unity of me is you. It's that simple.

Rise and shine, Queen!

HYGGE

HOLD *pure love in your heart to anchor the force of nature at higher levels.*

YOU *are the Y point of communication and redistribution.*

GENERATE *the full scale of the range of life experiences available to you. What will you create?*

GO *back in time to just before you encountered whatever still bothers you. Mentally undo and change things from there. Don't let anyone tell you that's not possible. Whatever happened at the point, let it go. Clean. Clean Clean.*

EMBRACE *your sovereignty. Declare it, and expand into the new, fuller version of yourself as a being with a whole different frequency range.*

THE HYGGE QUEEN

Subject only to Nature, she walks barefoot on the ground, one note in a symphony of sound. Anchoring Mother Earth Consciousness at the higher levels, she makes more space for her all expanding frequency.

Power tools:
Strong boundaries and consistent structure.

Archetype:
You, and everything you are.

REFERENCES

Chapter 15 Highway to Hygge
Kassem, S. (2011). Rise Up and Salute the Sun. Awakened Press. Retrieved from GoodReads: good-reads.com/quotes/tag/mother-earth Jacqueline, oraclegirl.org. J. (2021). A HIgher Biology - Track of the Month 4. Oracle Girl.

Chapter 16 Hygge Queen
Jacqueline, oraclegirl.org. J.-F. (2021, December 13). Track of the month 4. Retrieved from Oracle Girl: https://www.oraclegirl.org/library/track-of-the-month-4
Richardson, J. (2014, November 27). We are frequency vibration, and DNA is the antenna. Retrieved from Natural Life Energy: https://www.naturallifeenergy.com/frequency-vibration-dna-antenna/

EPILOGUE

So this is it – honey, roses, and happily ever after? Of course not – negative high-frequency beings have all kinds of trickery up their sleeves. Even so, their constant plucking on the sentimental harp of public heartstrings sounds increasingly tinny to me.

I thought I'd know it all by 62. Not true! If you're still alive at 95, you have things to do, experiences to ignite, lessons to burn.

Something new awaits you. I've realized few can describe nature, least of all me. I can only record how – since I reached out by jotting down my random musings – She opened my eyes, enveloped me with Her energy, and repatterned all my perceptions.

Believing I was separate from Her for even a second invariably led to pain. The more I whisper a resounding NO across the universe to anything threatening my connection with Her, the more loving, supportive, friendly frequencies flood back, enabling me to embody more hygge.

Ironically, as I jettison all inner and outer clutter to make more space for Her all-expanding frequency, any knowledge I need comes to me instantly.

Why would any multi-dimensional, all-powerful child of Nature seek advice or absolution from any alleged authority?

Sovereign beings need neither external management nor formulae. I answer only to the Earth's governing waters and the pure love coursing through my body.

It's all about the view. If you see Earth as just the environment, a separate entity from you, fear, separation, hate, and anger will likely be around you. When your viewpoint transcends all notions of being and non-being, creator and creature, you keep transmuting, repatterning, and generating anew.

I like to think of it all as a game. Things get more challenging as you move up the levels, but you'll be fine if you're sovereign, non-compliant, and operating from the inside out.

So what's the one essential thing you need to manifest anything? If you haven't guessed by now, that is your source connection – Mother Earth Consciousness, hygge, pure love, the gold frequency – call it whatever you like.

Plug into it, and you will always be on the highway to hygge. Hope to see you at the Coterie if you feel you're on the same bandwidth! Which reminds me.

Feedback is a super hyggelig thing to do, so please leave a review if any of this book resonates with you.

I'd be most grateful. Thank you!
Stay sovereign, Queens! Cheers!

GLOSSARY OF TERMS

A:

Affirmations: Entry-level spells that work for or against you.

Antenna: The visible component of wireless infrastructure. Our bodies are antennas that receive and emit fluctuating frequencies.

Our DNA's fractal antenna characteristics – electronic conduction and self symmetry – produce our life force with the movement of electrically charged particles within the body.

"The waters in your blood carry the gold frequency that turns your body into a live antenna broadcasting to all beings," says Jacqueline. "Once the gold frequency materializes in your blood constituents, you can connect to all beings and the universal mainframe, rather than the old system's societal setup that hacked our realm.[1]

Attention: Prana for corporates and other entities reaching out to you.

B:

Biofield: the energy field that surrounds all living things.

Electromagnetic patterns or vibrations within the human torus-shaped biofield relate to our emotional and physical states.

Nobel Prize Laureate Professor Murray Gell-Mann has shown quantum cellular fields govern body chemistry.[2]

Biofield Tuning: Using tuning forks to restore systemic balance.

Body-Mind Reality: A combination of mirror images reflecting multiple signal-emitting identities that create our reality through attraction or repulsion. Repatterning occurs when those pictures and their corresponding identities burn up in transmutation.

---

1   Jacqueline, oraclegirl.org 2021
2   Sorensen, 2017

C:

Colonists: Settlers or founders of a colony. In this context, the supposition of an invisible presence below Earth. For centuries they merged their DNA with people in high places to overcome their inability to thrive above ground for long.

Their use of technology, including the "science of images,"[3] to control humanity is their biggest strength.

Genetics – introduced via science, medicine, and technology – enable them to produce hybrid humans with bodies similar to ours. They aim to make human genetics even more susceptible to their influences.

Think politicians who roll out the rules and laws. See *negative high-frequency beings.*

Consciousness: A mixture of purifications and patterns that pertain to density.

Constructive interference: Tangling vibrations gain more power, aka 'good vibes.'

Cult: Any situation in which you are not allowed your own opinions or to come and go as you choose.[4]

Cymatics: the study of wave phenomena, especially sound, and their visual representations.[5]

---

3   Oraclegirl.org The science of images collection August 22 2021
4   Oraclegirl.org, Cults and Crazies, February 26, 2022
5   Collins Dictionary, n.d.

F:

Future Re-write: The mechanism by which your total grasp of a situation or human experience enables you to cancel or transmute it.

Frequency: The note beneath your thoughts and emotions encompasses several bandwidth ranges and rings out across the universe. It does not change according to your experiences, as your feelings belong to an identity. So whether you're sad or happy, your frequency remains the same.[6]

G:

Global Nature Intelligence System: – the body log of all of the frequencies and coordinates of how you purify the patterns inside and around you.

Gold Frequency: Your antenna's live wire – "the super information highway coursing, computing, and tabulating the collective human experience that switches on your self-healing abilities, activates your purifying instructions, and deletes the slave self."[7]

Green values: A rebranding of the old slave-trade consciousness that continues to traffick human data as commodities, hijack the Earth's resources, and force people into a way of being under the weaponized umbrella of pseudo-political terminology.

H:

Hygge: More than coffee and cake, hygge is the ultimate nourishment within an expansive free realm of 'give and take.'

---

6   Jacqueline, oraclegirl.org 2021
7   Jacqueline, oraclegirl.org 2021

I:

Infinity Spark: The creative, atomic part of your sun connection that emits the golden pure love frequency.

Inner being: The deeper invisible aspect of you that is always present but not yet seen.

Intuition: Empathic resonance as your body integrates, assimilates, and taps into frequencies that connect your state of awareness with the unseen. To interpret the integrity of the information, you keep turning the dial until the static sounds become clear. Learn to listen with your inner ear.

J:

Junk DNA: There's no such thing. The four million gene switches in DNA, once dismissed as junk, control the behavior of cells, organs, genes, and other tissues, with a second, secret DNA code.[8]

M:

Mass Formation Psychosis: A condition for totalitarianism, when a large part of society focuses on a leader(s) or a series of events. Followers can be hypnotized and led anywhere, regardless of data proving otherwise.[9]

Me: A human node – an intersecting redistribution and communication point that emits and receives energy from my internal and external environment.

Mind: Your mind is an application running in your body's operating system. A receiver for the intelligence of yourself and nature. To be

---

8   Copac, 2017
9   SWFI , 2022

mindful (cognizant) is to look after or care for something, an embedded concept shared by plants and humans. Psychotropic plants can facilitate the transmission of knowledge to humans.[10]

N:

Negative High-Frequency Beings: Another word for the colonists, a body-less predator that came to Earth long ago and infiltrated human consciousness via thought. Their slave-self body technology enabled them to emerge, splice themselves and take over humans. Many manifest as narcissists or sociopaths feeding on anger and fear, unable to discern between love and the other system.

Not me: Multiple slave-self identities and personalities that developed from tuning into Colonist frequencies.

Node: The time-space coordinate that turns up in material form. You, as a node, provide a placement, positioning, or marker that functions as a routing point for consciousness and the hookup of the gold frequency at a place where others can connect with themselves.
You individuate that mainframe. That's why you look different from every other person.[11]

O:

Organic portal: "A subtly constructed reflex machine that can perfectly mimic human personality."[12]

P:

Pure love: A passion that burns, transmutes, and regenerates anything superfluous.

---

10   Addams, 2022
11   Jacqueline, oraclegirl.org 2021
12   Cleckley, 1988

Prana: A plasmic patina-essence built over time. An unseen energy exchange according to the vibe or mood people give off. An object, given a certain cachet, will exude prana. We have a finite amount of prana, so it's essential to recognize where it's going.[13]

S:

Self-healing ability: Part of the Pure Love frequency, encountering others with strong self-healing abilities helps you accelerate yours.

Shielding: Distinguishing your energy from the feelings of others.

Sound Balancing: A syntropic process of bringing lost life force back into our bodies.

Sovereignty: Your inner intelligence system is your sole source of information, and you are subject to nobody.

Spirituality: Interchangeable with religion, it's a poor substitute for sovereignty.

Source connection: Light, constancy, and potentiality.

T:

Two Suns: Your inner sun appears in two forms connecting you with the gold frequency. The first sun purifies. The second plays a part in how you upgrade your body, bringing about materialization through your unique six-elemental setup.[14]

---

13   True, 2020
14   Jacqueline, oraclegirl.org 2021

REFERENCES

Addams, M. (2022, March 1). Retrieved from Twitter: https://twitter.com/sabri44220662/status/1498421761846693895?s=20&t=g3fjN3NjsV0Pwe-RaCRQDA

Collins Dictionary. (n.d.). Retrieved from collinsdictionary.com/dictionary/english/cymatics

Copac, D. (2017, November 29). Scientists Finally Admit There Is a Second, Secret DNA Code Which Controls Genes. Retrieved from Qwaym.com: https://www.qwaym.com/scientists-finally-admit-second-secret-dna-code-controls-genes/

Jacqueline, oraclegirl.org. (2021, December 17). Track of the Month 4.

Jacqueline, oraclegirl.org. (2022, February 27). Cults and Crazies. Retrieved from Oracle Girl: oraclegirl.org (2021, December 17).

Sorensen, S. (2017, February 9). Evolution of Bio-Energetic Medicine.
Retrieved from futurelifescience: https://futurelifescience.com/evolution-bio-energetic-medicine/

SWFI. (2022, January 2). What is Mass Formation Psychosis?
Retrieved from SWFI: https://www.swfinstitute.org/news/90470/what-is-mass-formation-psychosis

True, J. (2020, June 16). James True explains Prana.
YouTube: https://www.youtube.com/watch?v=q-vo_FAIxtU

ABOUT THE AUTHOR

International media award-winning travel journalist Caroline Hurry's work has appeared in *Independent Newspapers*, *The Citizen*, *Sunday Times*, *Business Traveller*, *Habitat*, and *A SMALL WORLD*, among other publications.

A cat slave, dog wrangler, and keeper of chickens, she is married to a Dane, and the hyggelig culture of that Scandinavian country is close to her heart.

Reign: 16 Secrets From 6 Queens To Rule Your World With Clarity, Connection & Sovereignty is her second book.

PRAISE FOR REIGN

This book is part Shakespearean play, part beautiful lyrical poem that introduces you to fierce and powerful women, each of whom embarked on a hero's journey to triumph in her own life. The fact that the author could have known so many queens with so many fantastical stories tells you a bit about who she must be as a human being. But I think she would say that every woman is a queen because every woman has triumphed in her own life.

There are magical queens in our midst. I dare you to ever look at another woman the same way after reading this book.

YVONNE AILEEN
Author of Goddesses Don't Diet:
The Girlfriends' Guide to Intermittent Fasting.

The depth of Caroline Hurry's poetic narrative is raw and authentic. She illuminates our deepest insecurities in prose that bruises as much as it uplifts.

Her courageous journey and those of the women she writes about in Reign resonated on so many levels. An astounding body of literary work.

JANINE LAZARUS
Author of Bait

What an extraordinary book! Caroline has been weaving magical word spells, and this is the culmination of decades of wisdom and observation. No one understands the human psyche quite as well. Caroline makes me laugh out loud at our absurdities. She teaches me things I didn't realize I needed to know. It would be a crime to miss her beautifully-written new masterpiece.

LINDA SHAW
Author of Horoscope Hotties

Reign inspires you to bask in the type of self-love no romantic attachment can equal. This moving elegy to nature could not have come at a better time in our lives. Expect the unexpected in this exhilarating train ride of a book.

LANA JACOBSON
Author of Ribbons of My Life

233